PORT ARTHUR
28th APRIL 1996 ...
AND THE AFTERMATH

A Personal Account

PETER HAZELWOOD

PORT ARTHUR - 28th APRIL 1996 ... AND THE AFTERMATH
A Personal Account
Text copyright © 2017 Peter Hazelwood
Cover image copyright © 2017 Andrew Tilt

Formatted by Lilly Pilly Publishing, 2017
lillypillypublishing@outlook.com

Lilly Pilly
PUBLISHING

ISBN: 978-0-6481425-0-8 (print book)

All Rights Reserved. No part of this publication may be reproduced, stored in, or introduced into a retrieval system, or transmitted, in any form, or by any means (electronic, mechanical, photocopying, recording or otherwise) without the prior written permission of the author. pandkhazelwood@bigpond.com

Cataloging-in-Publication data is available at the National Library of Australia

This book is dedicated to Nicole Burgess
- Koonya, Tasman Peninsula.
29 August 1978 – 28 April 1996.
Daughter of John and Sue, sister of Danielle
- Forever Young.

INTRODUCTION
By *Andrew Tilt*
Former Chief of Staff to Tasmanian Premier Robin Gray, 1982-88.
Launceston, 2017.

We were lucky enough to lure Peter Hazelwood to Tasmania in 1987, winning him away from the hectic Sydney radio scene to the slightly calmer world of politics in the Gray Liberal Government. It was a gain for the state: the whole family adapted comfortably to their new environment and Peter went on to make a great contribution in a variety of different media roles.

As a seasoned political journalist, Peter's career began in talk-back radio in Sydney in the seventies, extending to bureau chief and political correspondent in Parliament House, Hobart; media policy adviser and Premier's press secretary for three Tasmanian Liberal Governments in the eighties and nineties, and more recently adviser to the Shooters and Fishers Party holding balance of power in the NSW Upper House before moving to Queensland as an adviser in the state political arena.

He also developed an interest and active involvement in policing and security: as media adviser for a number of years for the Tasmanian Police Force, the Police Commissioner and SES; representing the Tasmanian Government on Commonwealth anti-terrorist organisations such as SAC-PAV; and contributing to the National Security Public

Information Guidelines booklet and the media component of the public document produced as part of Australia's National Counter Terrorism Response Plan.

Peter was press secretary to Premier Tony Rundle when the Port Arthur Massacre occurred on 28 April 1996. Alerted through his office on an otherwise quiet Sunday, he arrived on the relatively remote Police Forward Command post within hours of the tragic event.

Joining the Police Commander, for the next 24 hours Peter responded to the huge local/world media reaction whilst simultaneously advising the Premier and State Government Ministers on developments and appropriate responses.

Over the immediate and extended period subsequent to the shootings Peter was the State Governments "point man" for all media covering aftermath, public mourning, local social disruption and eventual trial of the perpetrator of the horrific crime.

Peter was awarded the Police Commissioner's Certificate of Commendation for his efforts at the Forward Command Post during the immediate period after that incident.

From a unique perspective combining his particular skill-set and being on location and attending aftermath events, Peter provides an insightful commentary on media and incident management of a terrorist-style event that now forms part of Australia's criminal history.

Drawn from Australia's largest mass-murder, his conclusions are as applicable today as they were then.

PORT ARTHUR
28th APRIL, 1996 ...
AND THE AFTERMATH

A Personal Account

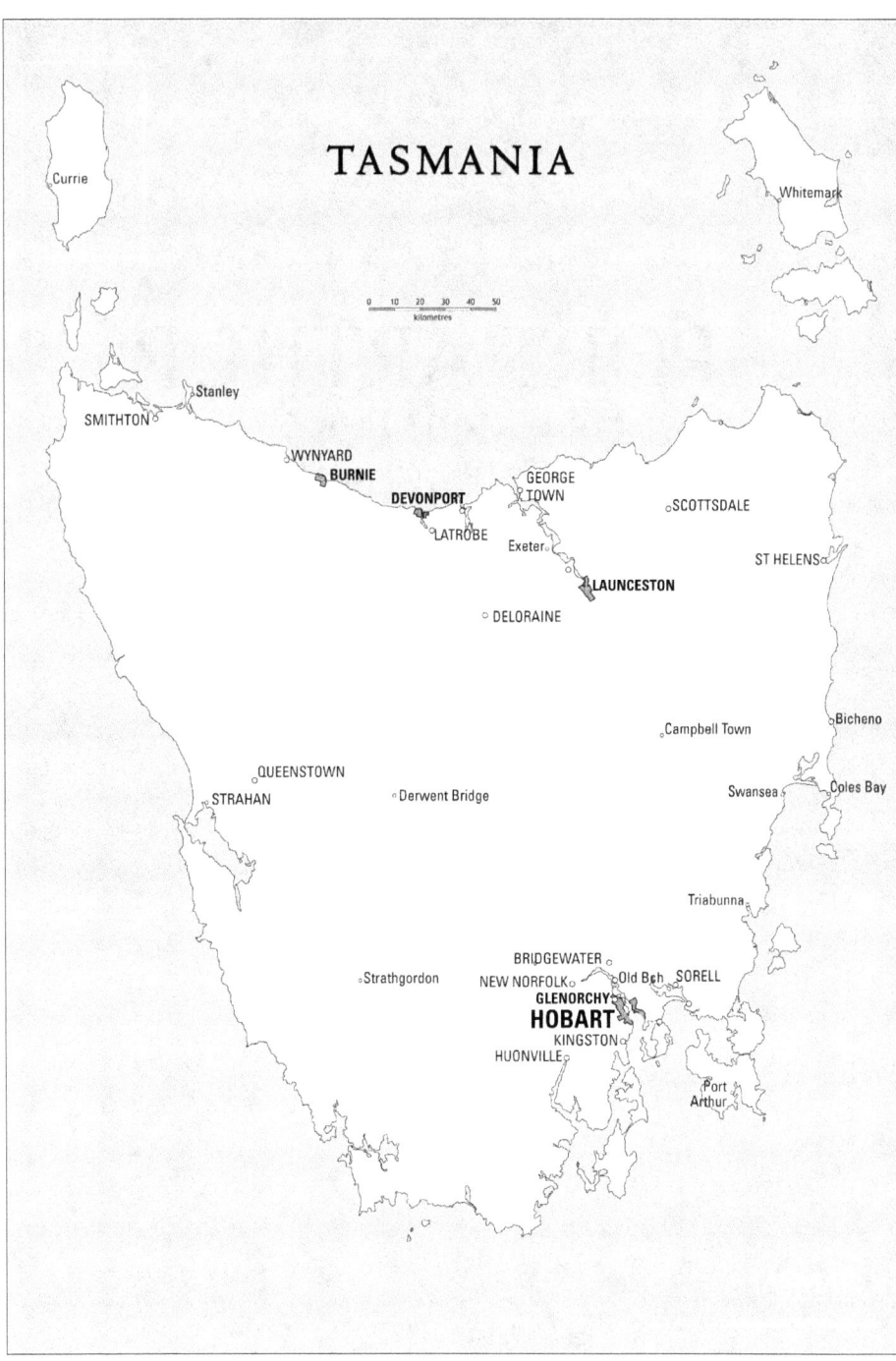

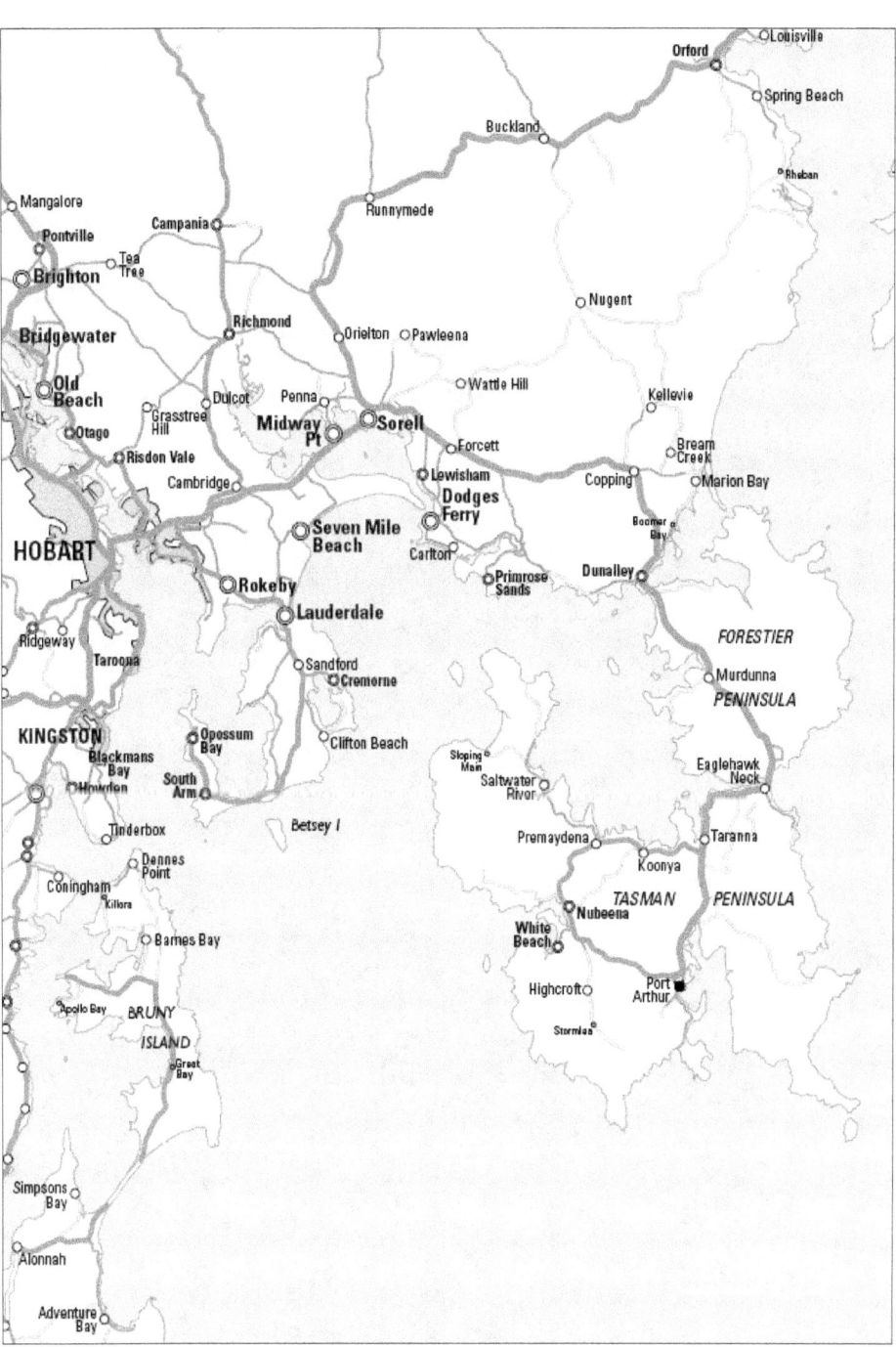

Contents

28th APRIL, 1996
THE DAY OF FORTY HOURS 1

TUESDAY 30TH APRIL, 1996
AND THE REST OF THE WEEK 56

THE RECOVERY PROCESS 91

THE TRIAL OF MARTIN BRYANT 111

THE SENTENCING OF MARTIN BRYANT . . 180

SOME REFLECTIONS 203

28TH APRIL 1996
The Day of Forty Hours

Everyone who was in Tasmania at the time has a Port Arthur story – I am no different except that perhaps I was involved more closely and for longer than most.

Like many others, I can remember exactly what I was doing and what I did on that day and many of those following this obscene massacre of thirty five people on 28th April, 1996.

That day started for me as it had for virtually every Sunday morning in the previous six months, with a visit to Hobart's maximum security prison at Risdon. The man I was visiting was, until 1.30 pm on that day, Tasmania's most notorious killer, Jack Newman, also known as Rory Jack Thomson.

The visits were usually from about 10am until about 11.30 am where we talked about all manner of things scientific, personal, gardening and generally I thought, gave him a break from the routine life of a hospital patient/prisoner in a maximum security hospital facility.

I first met Jack after Sarah, my eldest daughter, for some reason decided to use his case as part of a legal studies course at

High School – she wrote to him and then wanted to visit the prison hospital to talk to him. Not wanting her to go alone, I went as well – and, after that first visit, just seemed to keep going back.

Newman was not a convicted criminal as such – he killed his wife. He was found not guilty of the particularly brutal murder of his wife on the grounds of insanity. Jack thought that by using that plea, he would do some time in jail, and then be found to be 'cured' and released. He didn't count on just how those particular cases are dealt with by politicians.

I think his case has similarities to that of Graham Gene Potter, who pleaded not guilty but was convicted of the murder of Kim Narelle Barry in Wollongong, at about the same time as the Newman case. The difference is that Potter has long since been released from prison after serving his time for murder.

Newman, although having had four favourable Mental Health Review Tribunal reports, was ignored by politicians because as the law stood in 1996, it was they who had to decide if they believed the Tribunal recommendations and set him free.

But that is a whole new area for discussion in some other forum, or would have been had not Jack committed suicide in his cell early one morning in September, 1999. He used the long shoelaces from his gym shoes to form a noose which he tied to an air conditioning unit in his cell and strangled to death.

Jack was a totally flawed human being and probably would never have again fitted into society, but I feel he was badly let down by the system and some of those who were charged with his care.

A few months before his death he did manage to wander away from the prison, in what was described as an escape attempt – it may well have been but I think it was more a move of desperation. Jack was convinced he was never going to be released from the prison hospital, and the positive Mental Health Review Tribunal findings which were ignored by the politicians would tend to back him up.

But the cruelest thing of all was the fact that when he was returned to the prison after the 'escape', he was treated as a maximum security prisoner, rather than a maximum security hospital patient. Not only was he no longer allowed outside the prison's main fence, to do the gardens as he had been previously, he wasn't even allowed out of the hospital to do the gardens inside.

And for a person who had survived about 17 years in an institution, mostly by concentrating on his gardening activities, this was the worst thing they could have done. But they did – and now he is dead.

It was out of character for Jack to kill himself because he told me early on when I started visiting him, and asked him about suicide, that "he could have done it anytime since he was locked up, but had no intention of doing so". And I must admit that I was as surprised as anyone to hear that Saturday in September, 1999, that he had killed himself.

A coroner's inquest was held during May-June, 2000, and it was interesting to read what the comments in relation to Jack were.

Counsel assisting the inquest, Simon Cooper decided Risdon Prison psychiatrist, Dr Alan Jager, contributed to the death of prison hospital inmate Jack Newman. Mr Cooper said several psychiatrists agreed Newman suffered a major depressive episode after his escape attempt, but Dr Jager disagreed. Mr Cooper said this was significant because it determined Newman's treatment and medication.

On 15 September, Newman asked to see Dr Jager, citing his overwhelming remorse and guilt at past actions and saying he needed to resume his garden privileges to occupy his mind.

Mr Cooper said Dr Jager saw the request but did nothing. On September 18, Newman, then 57 years old, was found hanging in a hospital cell. Mr Cooper said Newman's death highlighted Dr Jager's inexperience and the need for a second psychiatric opinion to be available in the hospital.

All well and good, but Jack is still dead.

But back to April 28, 1996 – for many Tasmanians it is a bit like the moon landing or the assassination of John Kennedy – everyone can remember where they were when they first heard about the Port Arthur killings.

I put these words down on paper mostly from my own involvement and knowledge of the entire event, but have also drawn on some official reports and court records to provide finer detail. It is not meant to be the definitive Port Arthur story, rather my own personal recollections of being involved in what tragically is now part of Australia's history.

At the time I was Press Secretary to the newly elected Premier of Tasmania, Tony Rundle. It was my weekend for media duty and on that Sunday I was in the office about 1 pm doing some work for the coming week. I remember it being a beautiful autumn day and in fact resented having to be in the office at all.

It was about 1.50 pm when Tim Sauer, the Senior Private Secretary to the Attorney General, Mr Ray Groom, called my mobile to tell me that there was apparently "some sort of disturbance or incident at Port Arthur, and that several people had been killed" and asked had I heard anything?

I told him that I hadn't but that I would make some calls. Then all hell started to break loose. Next I called Geoff Easton of Tasmania Police Public Relations – he hadn't heard anything either, but would also make some calls.

In the meantime, I called the Premier at his home in Devonport and told him that it appears we have up to a dozen people dead at Port Arthur, but I cannot tell him why or how they are dead.

He was about to leave for Hobart for Parliament in the coming week, and unlike many people in high places, he was going to drive himself and his wife in their own private car, and would not have the normal access to his mobile phones for the three hours of the journey.

On hearing about the unfolding tragedy, Tony, like all of us just getting involved in this massacre, was non-believing and tried to rationalise what had happened. His and my immediate speculation was a bus accident or a boating tragedy, but disbelief was the immediate reaction.

He said he would delay his trip for a few minutes to see if I could get more news for him.

Next I got a call back from Geoff Easton who was now able to say that police were working on information about a man going mad with a gun at Port Arthur and that at least twenty-two people were dead.

He then went to the Police Operations Centre in Hobart to join the officers who were already setting up what is known as the State Crisis Centre or Major Incident Room to deal with the unfolding catastrophe.

I called the Premier back and told him the updated news.

He was silent for a second – again disbelief – and immediately changed his plans and organised to fly to Hobart so as to be there as soon as possible.

The next call I received was from Darcy Tronson, Head of the Premier's Office, who was now also in the loop. We swapped information and it was decided that I should get straight down to Port Arthur to 'handle the media'.

Fortunately in Australia we had at the time, a group known as the Standing Advisory Committee on Commonwealth-State Coordination for Protection Against Violence, or SACPAV for short. I think it is now known as the Counter Terrorism Committee or some such, but it is still the same animal playing by the same rules.

SACPAV came into being after the Hilton Hotel Bombing in 1979 to ensure (from then on) nationwide readiness and cooperation in order to protect Australia from politically motivated violence, including anti-terrorist hijacking measures and to provide for VIP protection. It involves relevant Federal, State and Territorial government departments; police services, and when appropriate, the Defence Force.

As part of this program, Tasmania was required to maintain 30 fully trained police officers equipped to respond to any incident of politically motivated violence that may arise. Members undergo regular training in the use of special equipment and take part in annual national exercises to validate their effectiveness. SACPAV was a godsend to Tasmania in the next 24 hours.

Martin Bryant was not a terrorist in the normal sense of the word, but because I had been involved in SACPAV and so had many of the police and public servants in Tasmania, that was how we responded.

I called my wife, Kris, at home. By now the time was probably 2.30 pm, an hour after the mayhem began. I told her to "put together some clothes that were warm because I was having to go to Port Arthur where someone had shot at least twenty-two people, and that I may have to stay overnight". Little did I know it would be 26 hours before I was able to get home again.

She, like everyone else, was dumbfounded – total disbelief that this could happen, and in Tasmania of all places. And she was immediately concerned about why I had to go, and how close I would be to the action at Port Arthur.

At this time we had an Army reservist friend visiting and he instantly recognised the gravity of such an event and began making calls to see if the Reserves may be called out to help in the situation.

I must have been thinking fairly clearly at the time, despite the enormity of what was unfolding, because for some reason I got Kris to throw a pair of gum boots in as well. Tasmania can be very cold at night, but also very wet, and I had no idea just where I was heading to at Port Arthur, but knew we could be going anywhere, with some or no facilities at all.

And that was how it turned out – in the end the gum boots weren't needed but I didn't have nearly enough warm clothes, nor did most of the media who ended up there with me that night.

By way of historic background, from the earliest days of settlement of the island, the Tasman Peninsula was identified as an ideal location for a prison from which escape by land or sea was impossible. A 400 odd metre strip of land at Eaglehawk Neck was easily protected by savage dogs chained at intervals and the coastline was so rugged that escape by sea really didn't come to mind.

The former convict settlement at Port Arthur is Australia's most significant heritage site. Between 1830 and 1877, it housed 12,500 convicts, their guards and free settlers. Convicts who died there were buried on the Isle of the Dead, in the middle of the Harbour off the penitentiary.

The gardens of Port Arthur are notable as a record of the 1830's. From that time, plants collected from around the world were added to plantings of Oaks and Ashes and other favoured English trees. All garden sites have survived intact to this day and a works program is continuing to restore the 19th century features, including paths, walls and fences.

In short it was a quaint place for tourists to visit. That image was being shattered forever this Sunday afternoon.

Even as I left the office in the centre of Hobart to go home and pick up the few things I thought I might need, the city streets were being closed off by police to allow ambulances direct and urgent access to the hospital from the helipad on the nearby Domain.

The first of the helicopters with seriously injured patients on board was being unloaded at eighteen minutes past three and the second one was just nine minutes later. The pilots then made the return flight to what was in all sense of the words, hell on earth.

The Premier, who by now was on his way by air from Devonport to Hobart had already decided that the media should be provided with as much information and assistance as practical and possible in the coverage of this shocking tragedy. I think all of the media who came to Tasmania that week will agree that the co-operation they received was unlike any they had previously experienced on major stories.

Tony Rundle of course was formerly a journalist himself and instantly recognised the impact these murders would have, not only on Tasmania, but nationally and internationally.

That decision by the Premier was one that helped Tasmania recover, more quickly than it otherwise might have, from Port Arthur. It showed we were transparent and keen to co-operate despite the enormous tragedy that was unfolding.

The drive to Port Arthur that afternoon should have been pleasant – the day was wonderfully clear and sunny but there was a sense of disbelief about what I was going to.

I had been involved in SAC-PAV exercises on an almost annual basis since arriving in Tasmania in 1988, unknowingly at the time, in preparation for this exact situation. Within the first few minutes of this massacre becoming obvious, my mind went straight into exercise mode. That is, I started thinking that if this was an exercise, what would I, as Media Liaison Officer for this exercise, do next?

In hindsight, I must say that it was by going into this situation with the thought of it being an exercise that helped to keep me going. The longer it went, and the worse the death toll became, the more difficult it was to think it was real, because if you could keep a little detached, you could function much better and be of more help to the people at the scene, and that was the immediate need.

Because of SAC-PAV, I knew that the police would have established a Forward Command Post somewhere near where Bryant had gone to ground after the shootings. It was at the Seascape Guesthouse. I knew that if I kept going towards Port Arthur I would find it.

Within an hour of leaving Hobart I arrived at a police road block at Taranna, just six kilometres north of Port Arthur. This was at a junction in the Highway. The road straight ahead went to Port Arthur. By going to the right, you went to Port Arthur via Nubeena. The Police Forward Command Post had actually been set up formally by ten minutes to four by Inspector Peter Wild.

It was a strange feeling heading towards Port Arthur, because looking back now I remember there was no traffic going in the opposite direction to me that is, from the Peninsula heading back to Hobart. Not one car passed me on the way to Port Arthur either, most likely because it was necessarily a very quick trip on the day. Port Arthur is an isolated community and the road was renowned for being treacherous. It is narrow and it is winding and around any corner you could find a loaded log truck or some sort of native animal. It was normally a 90 minute trip, at best. On this Sunday I think I covered the distance in a little over an hour.

The reason for the lack of traffic back to Hobart, I found out soon after, was that very few vehicles were able to actually leave Port Arthur because the gunman had still not been positively contained. All traffic was being stopped at the Koonya turnoff at Taranna, only local residents were being allowed through as far as Nubeena. The police had begun setting up the Forward Command Post in the reception area of John Hamilton's Tasmanian Devil Park tourist attraction.

There was not yet chaos in the area, but it was not far away, and with night falling, it promised to be an almost unmanageable situation from all viewpoints.

Superintendent Barry Bennett was the officer in charge of the Operation at the Forward Command Post. On identifying myself to police as being from the Premier's Office, and that I was available to act as Media Liaison Officer, I was taken to him inside the Command Post and welcomed with open arms.

The situation was a serious as it could get. Barry had enough problems in dealing with the massacre incident, which was still unresolved and because there was still some doubt as to whether Bryant had actually been run to ground; without the added burden of also worrying about keeping the media happy.

His immediate reaction was marvellous as far as my job as media officer was concerned.

"Thank God you are here. Just tell me what you want for the media and when you want it and I will do it," he said.

Fortunately, Superintendent Barry Bennett and I had been involved in a number of earlier SAC-PAV exercises, and while no words on the issue were spoken between us, I think we both assumed that the best way to handle what we were involved with would be to follow the SAC-PAV guidelines.

That way, I knew what to expect of him, and he knew what to expect from me, and that was how it actually worked through that long night.

He told me that he had spoken briefly already to the media

that were there to get stories for the 5 pm news bulletins; but would, wherever possible, do whatever was needed for as long as was needed.

At this stage, and bear in mind he was still trying to establish a Forward Command Post to direct what was the most important such operation of its type ever in Australia, Superintendent Bennett agreed to take a minute or two and talk to the media who were already on site.

We walked outside the office and, because the media was mostly local, and they knew me from my political role, it was an easy job to get them together, and in fact ask them what they needed and set out some guidelines for the next 24 hours.

To my embarrassment I actually introduced him as Inspector Bennett, rather than Superintendent, because I must admit I had missed his promotion. He eventually rose to be Assistant Commissioner Bennett before retiring in 2002.

It was not ideal to have the media assembled in the car park of what was the Forward Command Post, but the decision was made, early, that it was impractical to try to separate them from the immediate area and perhaps move them back to the local bakery about half a kilometre away.

The way it happened on the day was that media and police were arriving on the scene at the same time, and the fact that the media got mixed up with the Special Operations Group officers as they arrived could not be helped.

As I said, the situation in regard to the media being so close, in fact within the perimeter of the Forward Command Post, was not ideal, but now was a fact of life and we just had to work with it.

That quick initial briefing and updating of the situation covered the media for their next news bulletins at 6 pm that Sunday night, and so there was no more immediate pressure from them because they had all there was to be had at that stage.

As Media Liaison Officer that day, I was most fortunate to have Barry Bennett as commanding officer for the first twelve hours – an officer without his view of how to handle the media could have seen an entirely different situation develop over the next day. And the results would have been much different as well.

There was marvellous co-operation from most of the media that night, and Barry told them at his first briefing that he would do what he could when he could, and asked would it be suitable to them to have him come outside every hour to brief and update them on the situation. He was disarmingly upfront with them and they appreciated his openness.

I don't think that, until this point, in any similar situation, anywhere in Australia, that an officer at a Forward Command Post was so open and so willing to handle and deal with the media. But then, let's face it, there had never been a similar situation to this anywhere in Australia.

And that was the way it happened. About every hour, all through that long night of 28 April, 1996, I would bring Barry out to the media for an update of the situation that was unfolding.

However, one early blemish on the media performance at Port Arthur had already occurred. *ABC Radio* in Hobart, through reporter Alison Smith, had already done what the media around the nation had agreed not to do years earlier after the infamous Kangi Angi (NSW) fiasco with *A Current Affair*, where they talked to the villain staging a siege.

Smith knew, I assume from police radios, that Bryant was in Seascape Guesthouse, so did what she was not supposed to, and rang the house.

Bryant answered and Smith had her scoop – what she didn't know was that the phone Bryant was using had a battery; and that battery only had a finite life that night. Her call was not a long one and didn't really add much, if anything, to the overall story, but did breach the alleged code agreed to by the Media Entertainment and Arts Alliance; and it did mean that police had less time in which they could talk to Bryant on that same phone later that night.

I personally believe the *ABC* claim that Smith made the call randomly; and that she didn't know she was calling the Seascape Guesthouse was nonsense. But I know she maintains it was purely accidental. Even worse, the police at the Forward Command Post were not made aware of the call until just before it was put to air in the 7 pm news bulletin.

After spending time talking to the media on site at Taranna, I went back into the Forward Command Post to assess the situation, insofar as what I would be doing for the night. The assessment didn't take long.

There were only two telephones at the Forward Command Post. Superintendent Bennett would need one to keep in touch with the Operations Centre in Hobart, and I thought that was probably the best use of the line as well. The other line would also best be used by police.

It didn't really matter in the first few hours because all the lines into and out of the Peninsula were blocked anyway, the system was basically in meltdown mode. Therefore there was no reliable means of communication for me to use to either keep in touch with Geoff Easton, the media officer in the Operations Centre, or my office in the Executive Building, or to talk to the media who could not get to Port Arthur.

The police radio system was also not very effective, and anyway was being monitored by the media and so was not secure. I was left with the mobile phone in my car, which did not work at the Forward Command Post, but which thankfully, did get a signal about three kilometres back down the road towards Hobart. Telecom technicians were already working to get more lines into the area, but that was not expected to happen until much later in the night.

All round, not an ideal situation, even for a SAC-PAV exercise, let alone the real thing.

The shootings had started at about 1.30 pm and by just after 5 pm, survivors, witnesses and day trippers began pouring out of Port Arthur and the chaos was palpable. They had to leave the back way, via Nubeena because the road past Seascape Guesthouse, was where Bryant had gone to ground. There would be a procession of vehicles leaving Port Arthur heading for Hobart for the next six hours.

I decided then, and by now it was about half past five, and I had been at the Forward Command Post for about an hour, that the best I could do was to look after the media already there to cover the story and provide briefings as regularly as possible throughout the night.

Back inside the Forward Command Post, officers were hastily trying to set up the tourist shop as a functional police operations centre. There seemed to be police everywhere – each having their own job to do and getting on with it despite the enormous logistical difficulties they were facing.

The known death toll at this time was, I think twenty-two – with more expected as police could move safely into the Port Arthur area. It was an horrendous toll to even contemplate, but it was real; it had happened and the killer was still not in custody.

With the media contingent satisfied for the moment, but growing by the minute with more local and mainland crews starting to arrive, I took the chance to get in my car and drive back down the road and make contact with several people. Since I arrived at the Devil Park about ninety minutes earlier, I had been unable to contact anyone back in Hobart.

Firstly I called home to let Kris and the kids know that I was OK, and that no, I wasn't near the shooting area, and that, yes, I would be careful and I would be safe.

Then I rang my office and got onto Darcy Tronson – I gave him a quick rundown on the situation as I knew it from my end. He had been briefed by the Police Operations Centre in Hobart and our information generally matched, which under the circumstances of poor communications, was a credit to the police officers in charge of this particular side of the operation.

That was only the first of my trips down the road that night. I was to make a lot more and because communications were poor, my vehicle also became the means for several of the journalists to be able to file their stories.

They appreciated the use of the car and the telephone. I appreciated their support for what Superintendent Barry Bennett and myself were trying to do both with them and for them.

As darkness fell, there was a frenzy of activity as more and more of the survivors and tourists who had been trapped at Port Arthur, until the police allowed them to leave en masse, started to arrive at Taranna.

The media pounced on each and every car as it came past the police road block. Cameras were shoved in windows, bright television lights were shone onto and into cars and questions by the dozen were shouted at the occupants. After what they had been through that afternoon, I don't know what they made of the media scrum they ran into that night.

Some were able to give brief descriptions of what happened. As you would expect, others were too shocked to say much, if anything at all, and others were very clear in what they could tell the world about the massacre.

But the media pursued them all relentlessly to the point where the police had to put a stop to cars being blocked on the road outside the Forward Command Post. The traffic jam they created was affecting the ability of the Special Operations Group and other police to actually get down to the Seascape cottages and do what they had to do.

When told not to stop the traffic outside the Command Post, but to go a bit further down the road, some of the media representatives spat the dummy and thought they were being blocked from getting more 'scoops'.

This is an occasion when those particular representatives were forgetting what had happened not far from them that day. There was no effort to prevent them talking to people. It was simply the police didn't want traffic blocking the way into and out of the Forward Command Post. The fact the media was told they could talk to people further down the road didn't satisfy them all.

The most prized possessions that night, apart from eyewitness accounts of what had happened, were photographs.

Cameramen from newspapers were bidding for undeveloped rolls of film from each tourist, promising all sorts of money. I understand one local freelance cameraman got hold of some film, quoted a price, and then handed the poor tourist a card with the name of a journalist on it. There was some real bargaining going on I can tell you. But it gets worse! That same cameraman then tried to sell the pictures back to the journalist, for double the price he had quoted the Port Arthur tourist.

That cameraman has, probably not surprisingly, since found it very difficult to get much freelance work in Hobart.

During all this, and as an indication of the cooperation Superintendent Bennett was prepared to give, he left the Forward Command Post to do a live cross to the 7 pm *ABC* television news. An hour earlier, reporter Andrew Fisher had asked if that was possible. Bennett agreed that unless mayhem erupted at the Seascape Cottages where Bryant was holed up, that it would be.

True to his word, at about ten past seven he asked if the *ABC* still wanted him, and so I went and asked the crew, and the answer was yes, at about 7.25 pm, so he could update the nation.

Now this was not an easy thing to do because the *ABC* had set up about three kilometres back down the road. It was the only place they could get their signal out.

A couple of minutes later, Barry walked out and I drove him in my vehicle back to where the *ABC* had set up. For a man dealing with what he was, Barry was enormously calm. He was thinking very clearly on many fronts at once, and said he realised it was important to work with the media, even if he didn't have a lot of new material to give them.

And so we drove out to a boat launching ramp on the edge of the bay and Barry went live nationally, updating the situation as he knew it to be. All he could do, really, was confirm the known death toll and the fact that a siege was underway and that sporadic shooting was continuing and attempts were being made to contact the gunman.

But it was the fact that he came out of the Command Post to do this interview at all that was the most important factor. Here was the officer in charge at the scene, telling people both locally and nationally what had happened, and what was being done about it. He surely was a reassuring authority figure at a time when people were still trying to come to terms with the enormity of the massacre.

After the live cross, it was back in the car and back to the Command Post. On the way I asked Barry if he wanted to call his wife and let her know he was OK.

He said no, she knew he was a policeman and it was the sort of thing police wives get used to.

Tragically, just under three years later, 16 Feb, 1999, Barry's son Ty, also a policeman, was killed in a car accident in the early hours of the morning while responding to a burglary call at Richmond just outside Hobart.

Back at Taranna, the Salvation Army had now arrived and set up their emergency food distribution truck outside the Devil Park office because there was literally nowhere else to put it.

To have the Salvos there that night was great, in that they supplied food and drink to the multitudes who otherwise would have gone hungry. But if we had to do it all again, I think we would try to relocate them somewhere else, indeed anywhere else.

To heat things and to cook they needed power, and to get that power they had a generator. I will never forget that noise which was there all night.

The death toll was steadily rising. It went from twenty-two to twenty-nine and then soon after to thirty-two.

I know that the new Australian Prime Minister Mr Howard had been in touch with the new Tasmanian Premier a couple of times in the previous hours, and was already in his own mind looking at what he could do about the massacre.

Mr Howard had only come to office on 2nd March.

He later told the SBS Insight program "... by the late afternoon and evening, and when I spoke to Tony Rundle, the Tasmanian Premier, he gave me a brief description of Tasmania's gun laws and we talked about what might be done and what could be done".

Police had now identified Bryant's car as the yellow Volvo abandoned near the toll booth entry gate at the Historic Site, and in that car they found a passport in his name.

However, there was still some uncertainty about whether it was Bryant acting alone, or someone who had stolen Bryant's car or whether there were actually two gunmen.

The media were briefed at 8 pm and again at 9 pm, but once the confirmed death toll reached thirty-two there was little new information to be provided.

The lack of proper communications between Taranna and Hobart made our job much more difficult than it needed to be.

During the night, the best informed reporter there was Ellen Whinnett, from the *Launceston Examiner* newspaper. She headed to the site as soon as she heard of the shootings and arrived about 6 pm.

Her contacts as a police reporter were remarkable and at one stage she was able to tell Bennett and myself two names of suspects in this outrageous event.

The names, at the time, were only available to the most senior police officers involved in the case, and so her information had to have come from within, which I admit, was a bit of a concern.

Bennett did not confirm or deny the names were the same as he was working on, simply sidestepping the issue saying it was too early to be discussing who may or may not be suspects, until the picture was clearer.

Part of a police round reporter's job is to establish good contacts, and Ellen had done her job well. There are times however that the journalists' 'good contacts' can inadvertently make it difficult for other police officers in the field, such was the case for Barry Bennett that night. He didn't need names being put into the public arena at that stage.

Ellen went on to work for the News Limited *Mercury* newspaper in Hobart and maintained her reputation as the best informed of all reporters on police and prison matters. She sometimes got stories before people would like her to have had them, but that is part of being a good journalist.

She eventually won a Walkley Award for a series of stories that saw the demise of a Tasmanian Governor, and when I last heard she was terrorising federal political staff in Canberra as the chief writer for the *Melbourne Herald Sun*.

If they haven't worked it out yet, my advice to them would be that if they are going to try to hide or withhold any information from her; or other reporters with contacts as good as hers, for any reason, just make sure that she doesn't already know it from somewhere else.

The betting will be, she is telling you the information, rather than asking you for it.

Bennett's task at Port Arthur that night was almost impossible at times. For instance, because of the lack of communications, he was at one stage sending down hand written notes to the Special Operations Group officers and they were sending back similar hand written messages.

This was taking up a great deal to time and just the notion of having to do this was fraught with disaster. Everyone no doubt remembers the old story about a commander sending a message to his officers asking them to send reinforcements we are going to advance, only to have it reach the other end as "send three and four pence we are going to a dance".

Fortunately, no such incident happened on this night, but the potential was probably there.

I remember about 11 pm that night driving back down the road to again make contact by mobile with my office, and this time Judy Tierney from *ABC* television also needed to make calls, so came with me.

I spoke to Darcy Tronson and we again compared notes on what was happening and what was likely to happen; and I brought him up to date with the growing media contingent and the fact that we had done about all we could that night.

I had made the mistake of not telling Hobart I was not alone in the car, and while the death toll at that stage was officially twenty-two, Darcy was just being given new information which took it to 29 – Judy had to simply sit in the car next to me and pretend she hadn't heard, and thankfully, she did. Judy then made her calls and we went back to the Forward Command Post, in time to hear Barry Bennett update the known death toll. Judy, thankfully appeared surprised, although clearly understanding the full magnitude of the still unfolding incident.

By about 11.30 pm, the media pack had reached its peak – there were crews from all the major newspapers, television stations and radio networks in Australia, and some from international services with Australian offices. They were all anxious for information and we tried our best to provide it for them.

Most accepted the fact that Taranna was as close as they would get to the Seascape Guest House that night. One newspaper photographer, and to our embarrassment, it was a local, decided he wouldn't accept the fact. He headed off, unbeknown to most people, overland towards Port Arthur.

I don't think he really knew where he was going, but the police managed to find him and suggest that he was out of bounds and should return to Taranna, either under his own power or theirs. He chose to go quietly and when he got back, magnanimously offered to tell the rest of the media that it was not possible to get closer to the scene that night.

But tomorrow was going to be a problem.

The local media were keen enough to do the right thing at Taranna. The nationals thought they could do what they wanted. They were backed by big money networks who encouraged them to do what they wanted, or I suppose from their point of view, do what was needed to 'scoop' the others.

This had the potential to cause enormous problems come

daylight and while no one was trying to censor the news in any way, we were attempting to manage the event in a manner that was suitable to all and advantaged no one over anyone else.

Interestingly enough, for a long time there was a different attitude towards the story between the local and national media.

The locals understood that behind every person who was listed as dead, and by now there were twenty-nine, were other people who would be affected by this tragedy. During the night, as more details emerged, they could put names and faces to the numbers and that made it real and devastating, on a personal level.

The national media were simply working on 'a great story' without regard, yet, for the people and personalities involved in the massacre.

This 'great story' attitude prevailed until about midday the next day when the police organised to bus everyone from the media who wanted to go, and they all did, into Port Arthur for a tour of the actual massacre site. That tour was what brought reality to the media who weren't already aware of it.

While walking about during the night and talking to the various crews I managed to pick up some good intelligence which we could act on to avert problems when daylight arrived.

Already in place was an air exclusion zone around the Port Arthur area, partly to keep media helicopters or other sightseers out of the area. We had a five mile zone, but I think with the development of even better long range cameras, any similar incident now would see a ten mile exclusion zone.

What we hadn't thought about until then was sea access to both Port Arthur and Seascape – but it only took a few minutes to have police impose a water exclusion zone as well. So the area was now sealed off by air, land and sea exclusion zones.

I suppose I really should apologise in particular to the Today program on the Nine Network for upsetting their original plans that night to head into Seascape by boat early on the Monday morning. Others were probably also planning similar moves, but they would have been foolhardy to say the least. Bryant wasn't armed with pop guns, and would have loved the chance to fire on media boats live on national television.

So when these exclusion zones went into place the area was again secure for when daylight arrived. It probably disappointed several locals who were set to make a fortune out of hiring their boats to the media, but in the interests of everyone's safety, the exclusion zone was the best option available.

We were to learn later, that local Nubeena Police Constable, Paul Hyland, and Constable Garry Whittle, had been the first police to reach the Seascape accommodation earlier in the day.

These officers got a message at about 1.30 pm to attend Port Arthur because of reports of shootings, and being some distance away at Saltwater River at the time, and travelling in separate vehicles, they called into the Nubeena station on the way to get further details.

There they got a message to be on the lookout for a yellow Volvo with a surfboard on roof racks. They decided to head to Port Arthur in different directions in an effort to locate the car.

Constable Hyland travelled to the Taranna turnoff on the Arthur Highway (where the Forward Command Post would be set up) and en route received a further message to look out for a gold coloured BMW sedan.

Once reaching the turn off, he got further information that people had been shot and were at the Fox and Hounds Hotel, just short of Port Arthur. He then drove south to the Fox and Hounds at considerable speed, observing on the way Linda White's abandoned Frontera on the roadway about a hundred metres past the Seascape entrance. I will have more on Linda's story later.

After speaking with the people at the Fox and Hounds he drove back in the direction of Seascape, and about 500 metres before the driveway, slowed down when he noticed Constable Whittle's vehicle approaching from behind him, and they proceeded slowly in convoy to the entrance gate.

Constable Hyland in fact decided to drive further north past the entrance to stop any traffic passing Seascape, and as he did, he saw a figure running past one of the cottages towards the entrance of the main residence of Seascape.

Stopping his vehicle across the roadway about 400 metres north of Seascape, he remained there for some time. Constable Whittle meanwhile had positioned his vehicle across the highway outside the Seascape entrance to block northbound traffic.

Shortly afterwards, Constable Pat Allen, reversed his police vehicle from the direction of Port Arthur towards Whittle's car. As he did so, Whittle heard three loud shots from the direction of Seascape and bullets passing over Allen's car hitting bush or shrubbery nearby. Whittle dived headfirst into a culvert at the rear of his car and was then joined by Constable Allen.

This pair remained in the culvert until about 9 pm that night, when they were joined by two members of the Special Operations Group; and were subsequently evacuated from that point at about 11 pm by crawling along the ditch, a distance of about 200 metres.

During their time sheltering in the culvert a large number of shots were fired in their general direction from several different weapons. As well as his own firearms, Bryant, after leaving Port Arthur, now had access to a considerable number of guns owned by the Martin family who ran the Seascape guest houses.

Constables Whittle and Allen, turned up at the Forward Command Post shortly after 11 pm, tired and cold and hungry and covered in leeches from their time in the culvert, but keen to continue on duty to support their fellow officers in the field. While they made no secret of the fact they had been in the ditch outside Seascape for many hours, the media that night never really picked up on the story. They did some time later, but for tonight they were concentrating on the death toll and where the murderer was holed up.

The briefings from Barry Bennett went hourly that night, until midnight when we called the media together and gave them the latest, which amounted to really what they already knew. That the death toll stood at thirty-two, that the Seascape Cottage had been surrounded and sealed off; that Bryant was still firing sporadically; and that all police efforts were being directed at ending the siege but that it was unlikely that anything further would happen that night.

We suggested that the media, who were also tired, get some sleep and there would be another briefing at 5 am on the Monday, to get them ready for their breakfast bulletins. There was also a promise and commitment from Barry that if anything serious happened before 5 am we would wake them all up and let them know.

This seemed to please everyone – and they headed off to their cars to try to get some sleep. Barry went back to his command post to deal with the dozens of problems he was facing.

The sporadic shooting from Bryant during the night was somehow targeting the Special Operations Group officers hiding in the bush and surrounding the cottages, and he was putting bullets very close to them in a pitch black night.

It wasn't until the whole thing was over that police worked out why he was able to do this. It wasn't because he had a night scope. He was, in fact, seeing the red glow from the transmission lights on their radios. Each time they clicked to send a message or reply to one, the light glowed, and Bryant fired.

While none of the officers were hit, they now know why he was able to get so close; and it has led to a change in procedure on how such lights are incorporated into police radios.

Through all the briefings that night, Superintendent Bennett did remarkably well to maintain his composure and good humour. There were some problems associated with the lack of communications from the Forward Command Post and the Police Operations Centre in Hobart.

It turned out that Hobart was releasing information and detail that Barry Bennett did not particularly want in the public arena at that time, and Hobart also was the source for the word 'schizophrenic' earlier in the night.

Bryant isn't and never was schizophrenic, but armed with that word from Hobart the media hammered Bennett a couple of times. It was something which nearly went down in folklore; that Bryant suffered the illness, and could easily have been the undoing of Bennett's credibility that night.

Another line of questioning that I found particularly upsetting was the insistence from one female reporter, I think from a mainland radio network, on knowing "how many children have been killed and how old were they" almost every hour.

The fact was, at that stage Bennett didn't want to canvass that detail. There was still a great deal of forensic work and indeed identification to be done and so he kept replying that "we have 22, 27, 29, 32 people confirmed dead at the moment, and obviously there is a chance that there may be some children involved".

Again, I think she was seeing more detail on information coming out of the Operations Centre in Hobart without the Operations Centre letting Bennett at the Forward Command Post, the pointy end of the operation, know just what they were saying to the media.

About half an hour after the last briefing of the night I was presented with another problem. A reporter from the Today program had somehow lied her way through the roadblocks earlier in the night and managed to get through to Nubeena and interviewed Neil Noye, the local mayor.

I say 'lied' because only residents, police and emergency services personnel were being allowed back towards Nubeena that night. No one identifying themselves as media was being permitted access. For heaven's sake, there have been thirty-two murders and the gunman is still not in custody.

Journalists, under their alleged code of ethics are bound to identify themselves as such in the circumstances that prevailed at the roadblock that night. If a lie wasn't told, then neither was the full truth offered. But be that as it may, she came back to the Forward Command Post, never admitting or volunteering the fact that she had been through to Nubeena, and begging for an interview with Bennett on the latest situation.

I had worked with Steve Leibmann on radio in Sydney some years ago and had maintained some contact with him. So in the interests of trying to do my job that night to the best of my ability, and to assist the media, I went back in and asked Barry if he would do it. Again he made the time and said he would be out in ten minutes.

Now, you can see what was going to happen – all the media who did the right thing have been sent to bed and have just about nodded off, in the knowledge that if anything at all happened they would be roused and told.

The minute the *Today* program crew turned on their lights, there would be mass panic from the 100 odd journalists and crew on site. So I had to quietly go around and tell as many as I could what was happening; and not to worry, there was no dramatic new development.

We got the interview underway and while I had told those I could, some crews still got edgy about the interview, thinking for a minute or two they were missing out or were being dudded.

But Bennett and I kept our word to act in good faith. I don't think this particular reporter had been, although she probably doesn't care now, either. She got her story and it probably made good morning television and it almost certainly made Neil Noye the voice and face of the Port Arthur tragedy for many people. I would only remind her again of the journalists' code of ethics under which I was trained, and it had a requirement that media representatives identify themselves as media, rather than sneak around roadblocks and such like.

I remember that it was about ten o'clock that night that two young paramedics arrived at the Forward Command Post. Both were quiet and unassuming and looked as if they had put in a hard day's work.

On this occasion, looks were not deceiving. Peter Stride and his partner that day, Warwick Allen, had literally been to hell and back.

They had been on the first helicopter into Port Arthur after the shootings – they arrived to be confronted with the devastation of what had happened.

During that Sunday night I spoke a lot with Peter when he wanted to speak and the point that stuck with me was a discussion about firearms.

Having been a shooter, and, in the past having had some sympathy with the gun lobby in their claims that legitimate shooters were being penalised and victimised because of the idiots, I proffered the comment that "no doubt when daylight arrives we will be faced with the anti-gun groups screaming that we need to ban all guns to stop this happening again, but he could have done this with any sort of firearm, couldn't he?"

The reply didn't take long and it was simple. "No, not what he did down there" and for a little while, he said no more, the look on his face said it all.

But when he did go on to reflect on where he had been and what he had been doing by way of medical assistance at Port Arthur in the previous seven hours or so, he left me in no doubt about who should and shouldn't in future have access to such firearms as were used that day.

The weapons Bryant was using at point blank range at Port Arthur, were a .308 calibre (7.62mm) and a .223 calibre (5.56mm). The first of these had a muzzle velocity of 838 metres a second, and the other was even higher with a muzzle velocity of 1000 metres a second.

Muzzle velocity is the speed with which the projectile leaves the end of the barrel. I leave it to you to imagine what damage that projectile does to a human body at close range.

Peter Stride's words that night were enough for me.

Meanwhile, Bennett was facing major logistical problems of changing shifts with his officers and organising the Victorian Special Operations Group members who by now were arriving from Melbourne, to back up and later replace the local officers who were surrounding Seascape. There were no problems with the officers, simply it was such a massive operation in less than adequate facilities in a less than adequate situation.

His headquarters had been set up quickly during the mid afternoon and by about 8 pm was functioning pretty well, given the circumstances.

Again those who were there had a job to do and did it, but they really were making the best out of a bad deal. To everyone's credit, there were no major glitches that were obvious to anyone.

Telstra technicians were marvellous in their efforts to organise a dozen or so new telephone lines into the Devil Park office. They did this by tapping into a nearby exchange and running the lines half a kilometre or so overland, and this gave added communications ability to a lot more officers and really helped smooth the operation.

At least I was able to use a landline telephone to communicate with my office in Hobart, and let them know what we had been doing; and also to see if anyone was planning what would happen with the media come sunrise. We had more than a hundred at Port Arthur, and there was probably just as many still in Hobart, who would want to get to Port Arthur as soon as they could.

Security became a bit of an issue during the night, because at one stage, a female reporter from Melbourne, who arrived very late at Taranna (it must have been nearly midnight), and took it upon herself to walk straight into the Forward Command Post and start reading information on what passed for whiteboards, and started to quiz officers on the detail.

She got a bit stroppy when it was suggested that she was in the wrong place; that the media were outside. From then on an officer was stationed at the door, but the incident highlights the problem of having the media too near the centre of operations.

Again this is not having a go at the media; no one was trying to keep anything from them. Simply it wasn't appropriate to have them wandering around in the middle of an operation of this kind, when all relevant information was being provided to them on the hour, outside.

It was sometime after midnight that I first met Neil Noye, the Mayor of Tasman Council, and the man who became the father figure of Port Arthur in the days ahead. It was not something Neil sought, but which was thrust upon him as community leader, and to this day I admire the way he handled what was a hell of a job.

But back to the night of 28th April, Neil had come into the Devil Park because the police were trying to work out ways of storming Seascape, if necessary.

He brought with him Council plans for the property, and the intelligence section of Tasmania Police immediately went to work with the Special Operations Group to work out how best to get into the building when and if the time came.

Part of the plan would obviously involve an approach to the house, and this was where there would be huge dangers because of the amount of weaponry and ammunition Bryant was known to have with him.

Initial thoughts, I think, turned to an armoured personnel carrier or something similar which the Army would have. Fact was though, the army in Tasmania did not have such a machine, and the logistics and time involved in getting one to Port Arthur from Victoria seemed to rule that out as an option.

The next thought then was for a D8 or D9 bulldozer, which of course has a large blade at the front, which could be raised to cover police behind it as it was driven towards the Seascape building. It was not the best plan in a perfect world; but this was not a perfect world, so improvisation was the key.

So poor old Neil was then asked if he knew anyone on the Peninsula who had such a machine, and almost instantly he came up with two or three possibilities and started making phone calls.

Remember that by now it was about 2 am on Monday, 29th April, but Neil began his calls.

The first couple could not help, but then he found a contractor who had a machine exactly like the one police wanted.

Neil went through the conversation in his own inimitable fashion and finally got around to asking if the dozer could be delivered on the back of a low loader to a point near Seascape.

It was then the contractor suddenly realised what Neil and the police had in mind, because Neil had until this point not given too much away about why he was ringing in the middle of the night and asking if this man had a bulldozer.

With the realisation that the machine was to be used, if necessary in a storming of the building, the contactor told Neil that certainly he could deliver the machine to the nominated point, "but you'll have to bloody well get someone else to drive it".

In the end the machine, I think, was delivered, although not needed. But amid the turmoil of the previous day and the long night, I thought that was one little bit of humour in an otherwise humourless day; and the response by the owner of the machine seemed to me to be typically, sardonically Australian.

The media crews had all settled for the night and I think many of them are indebted to Devil Park operator, John Hamilton, for supplying them with jumpers and beanies and other assorted clothing from his souvenir shop. It was a cold night and many media had simply been sent from home to cover this massacre and hadn't really thought of being out all night and didn't come dressed appropriately.

John didn't hesitate to get into his stock and supply whoever needed it with something warm – he also didn't ask for payment, simply told them to pay him the next time they were down at Port Arthur or post him a cheque when they got back to work – I hope they all did.

One point I still remember about Port Arthur (and I touched on it earlier,) which I need to expand on; and that was the initial difference in attitude of the media on site.

The local media knew that behind each and every fatality that day there were other human beings involved, and most likely local people from the Tasman area. Tasmania is a small state and it was also likely that some of the local media would know some of the dead; and that gave the story a much more forceful message than was being picked up on that first night by the national and international media.

As the media can sometimes do, they depersonalise incidents and treat them as 'good stories' rather than think too deeply about the human aspects of what they are covering.

Now I know it is not a good idea for the media to get personally involved in news stories, but it is equally not a good idea to treat tragedies simply as 'good news stories', there has to be some halfway compromise.

In fact, sometime after Port Arthur I was watching a television interview involving some journalists who had been covering the massacre and one woman offered the comment that she "liked being a journalist because you get to cover things like Port Arthur".

Now I don't know what she was meaning to say; but it didn't seem to come out appropriately for her if she really liked to cover stories such as this one, rather than go to such a story and provide honest, balanced and accurate coverage of the events.

With the media mostly tucked away in their cars trying to get some sleep, I found I couldn't. So for what was a very long night I walked about the car park and talked to those who were also awake and spent long hours in with Barry Bennett and his team as they kept planning for what was happening at Seascape and what would happen after daybreak.

All night long there was a stream of officers back and forward from Taranna to Seascape updating intelligence and providing other information which would help with planning for the next moves.

Police had lost contact with Bryant about 9 pm, when the portable phone he was using went dead – the batteries had apparently run out. While there were thoughts of trying to get him a second battery or another phone so contact could be resumed; the risk of exposing an officer for that purpose would have been tremendous and the idea was dropped.

Superintendent Bob Fielding arrived at the Forward Command Post about 4 am to relieve Barry Bennett, who had been there since about 3 pm the day before, and was given a detailed briefing on the situation at Seascape. He went over all the paper work available to fully acquaint himself with everything he needed to know.

With the media aware that the first briefing would be at 5 am, they started stirring about half past four and the car park again came to life. Not that it really went quiet during the night, but with the crews all now back on their feet it certainly was crowded. There was an air of growing anticipation. But no one really knew of what.

Because there was very little new to tell them, Barry went through what they already knew and suggested that again today it would be a waiting game to see what moves the gunman made, but that the whole situation was fluid.

It emerged during Bryant's trial in November, that during that Sunday night/Monday morning he fired in excess of 150 shots from various weapons at the police. The court was told that at no stage did any of the Special Operations Group police return fire because of the obvious risk to the hostages he still held.

Although there was nothing of significance in this briefing, the media still had the entire story to tell the nation as it awoke to the fact that one of the worst mass civil killings in recent Australian history had occurred in Tasmania.

It was after this first briefing on the Monday morning that one potentially disastrous idea was apparently being put in place in Hobart.

The first I knew of it was from one of the national media representatives who said he had heard that the media at Taranna had been ordered to go back to Hobart for a news conference to be held there at 7 am.

I dismissed it as not only untrue, but inadvisable and unworkable and went back inside to inform Superintendent Fielding of the rumour.

Barry Bennett was still in the process of handing over control to Bob when I told them of this story from the carpark and while I was joking about what a silly idea that would be, Fielding wasn't laughing with me.

He said he had been ordered not to talk to the media at Taranna about the situation happening just a few kilometres down the road at Seascape, but to tell the media, all 100 or so of them, to go 100 kilometres back to Hobart to hear about what the latest developments were.

I was dumbfounded.

The media had been told we would come out and talk to them again about 6 am, and it was now about 5.50 am.

The whole idea was unwise, if not ridiculous. I told Mr

Fielding that if we did have to tell them to go back to Hobart, the entire media contingent would rebel and simply break out. We would have no idea what they would do or where they would go. It would be mayhem and we would no longer be able to manage the situation.

Fielding to his credit however, like a good officer, said that he had been given an order and would follow it, just as he would expect anyone to whom he gives an order to carry out that order.

I felt a sudden attack of panic. This was never going to work and how the hell was I going to tell the media that they were getting no more briefings here at Taranna and that they should pack up and go all the way over the 100 kilometres or so of narrow, windy road on a trip of at least 90 minutes. Also it was not possible for them to leave now and get to Hobart before the conference started.

Let me say that at previous SAC-PAV training courses we were told clearly that during the Lockerbie disaster in Scotland, the media did not go to Edinburgh for their briefings, they went to Lockerbie.

Port Arthur would be exactly the same. There is no way the media would be in Hobart for information about Seascape.

So in quickly summing up the situation I said to Bob, "Come outside for a walk amongst the media, simply to stretch your legs and get some fresh air for the hours ahead when you don't know what will happen."

I said, "We could tell them it is still all quiet and that is why we are coming out before the 6 am scheduled briefing, because there is no real need for a briefing."

And that is what happened.

As ordered, Mr Fielding did not do the 6 am briefing. But he did wander about the car park while we both spoke about the need for fresh air and the fact that because nothing was happening at Seascape now was a good chance to take a break from the office. He also cleverly said to the media that, "because there was nothing happening would it be OK if he did not come out for another briefing until there was something significant to tell them?"

The media agreed that this was a reasonable suggestion and so that was the way we bought time until we could sort out what the hell to do.

Bob carried this off with an air of calmness that I wasn't feeling and we both went back inside the Forward Command Post. This was a situation which was about to burst out of control. I know I didn't need it, and Fielding needed it even less.

But then sometimes things do go your way. Shortly after we got back inside, one of my work colleagues, Adrian Lacey, who at the time was the Premier's Chief of Staff, (working as we all did under Head of Office, Darcy Tronson), turned up to see what he could do to help by way of giving me a break. It had been a long day since 2 pm Sunday, 28th April.

He was on his way to Port Arthur to help co-ordinate the media tour of the site later in the day, and about which plans had not yet been relayed to us at Taranna, but I will get back to that later. I told Adrian about what had been forced upon us that morning and his reaction was the same as mine, bullshit.

We went straight to a telephone and made a call to Darcy Tronson who was part of a special team which had been established on the Sunday night to oversee the entire disaster response operation.

It consisted of the Premier, Tony Rundle, Police Commissioner, John Johnson, Police Minister John Beswick, Secretary of the Department of Health and Community Services, Gillian Biscoe, the Minister for Health and Community Services, Peter McKay, and Secretary of the Department of Premier and Cabinet, Steven Haines.

In fact it was basically the Ministers and senior public servants of the agencies most involved or likely to be involved in the response to the murders and the aftermath. Its purpose was to let the front line people get on with doing their job, and it was an outstanding success. No doubt it will be the model for any future such disasters in Australia.

It also meant that major decisions could be made quickly and cleanly by these Department heads, and maybe other decisions which might not be in the best interests of everyone could be given further consideration and perhaps overturned if necessary.

Anyway, the situation I was in at Port Arthur was explained in fairly short measure and we were told to 'leave it with us', and so we did.

By now it was 7.30 am and yet another problem had arisen during the night. The toilets at the Devil Park couldn't cope with the huge influx of people and blocked up; we needed a plumber urgently. Silly muggins me decides that the quickest way to get one would be to go next door to John Hamilton's house and ask him to call in the plumber he uses at his tourist attraction.

So over I go and knock on the door – Mrs Hamilton opens it and for some reason, I still can't explain, except that I was getting very tired, I introduced myself and said I was from 'the

Media Office' without mentioning the word 'Government'.

She slammed the door in my face, saying she wanted nothing to do with the media. And there I stood, trying to talk through a door and explain that no, I wasn't from the media and that the toilets in the park were blocked and that we needed a plumber.

The door opened again, and it was John. He apologised and explained that the media were not popular at the moment because of the harassment that was already happening to people in some areas on the Peninsula the previous night and again already on the Monday morning.

In hindsight and knowing some of the things that did happen I understood their angst, and Mrs Hamilton's animosity towards the media.

But more importantly we needed a plumber, and so John went and organised that, much to the relief of all involved. It was shortly after this that the real action of the day started.

In the Forward Command Post word came through from the Special Operations Group that the house at Seascape was on fire. It was about 7.45 am, Monday morning.

This was where Bob Fielding turned in an incredible performance under unbelievable pressure.

And by the way, the phone call Adrian and I made earlier did lead to action.

Just as Seascape started burning, Fielding apparently got a call telling him to "go and talk to the media and keep them calm". He responded that he couldn't do that at the moment because he was busy, and so was then told, "send someone else out to talk to them and let them know the Deputy Commissioner, Mr McCreadie, was on his way down by helicopter to give them a full briefing" (which of course also meant they didn't have to go all the way back to Hobart).

As Fielding said in an aside to Adrian and I a little later, and during the unfolding of the end of the siege, "I don't know just where you blokes come from, but it must be pretty high up."

On my judgement, and to my relief, that reversal was the only sensible and realistic option and it avoided a lot of unnecessary problems between the police and the media that day.

Seascape guesthouse had been coded by the police so that references from police on the ground coincided with the plans on the main desk in the Command Post. By now, smoke was coming from all corners of the building and it could be seen from Taranna. Bryant was forcing the hand of the police. Do they go in and get him out or do they wait for him to come to them? Fielding was enormously calm as this drama began to play out.

He had to make many decisions, including what he thought was the likelihood of the three hostages still being alive and at what cost was he prepared to put police lives at risk to arrest this mass murderer.

Fielding obviously calculated that on the intelligence provided to him from those who had been listening to the house all night and had contact with Bryant the day before, and on everything that happened since the siege began, the hostages were dead. Just think of the gravity of that decision if it was one for you to make under the same circumstances.

Next, he had been told that in any attempt to storm the building, Bryant would be likely to kill at least five of the assault squad. In stark figures, in any assault he would most likely kill or injure thirty percent of the fifteen serving officers making up the squad. And the Special Operations Group officers I understand get paid only a couple of dollars a week extra to be part of the team.

Who would like to be in Fielding's shoes now?

In a calm and authoritative voice, Fielding ran the entire operation from the reception centre at the Tasmanian Devil Park.

Through radio contact from Seascape, the police reported the house to be burning from at least four points, and asked should they go in?

The answer was no.

Fielding had looked at the plans of the building and calculated that Bryant would be waiting for an assault and use his semi-automatic weapons to kill more people, in addition to the 35 he had already murdered. The senior police officer was not about to add police officers unnecessarily to the total.

The fire continued to burn and again the question was asked, do we go in? Again, no.

Police psychiatrists had predicted that Bryant would make what he considered to be a last heroic stand, and it would possibly involve fire; it was remarkable that they could profile this individual so well from having very little to go on.

Fielding kept his men outside and waited – he wasn't going to Bryant.

Bryant would have to come to the police, or burn. And so that was how it happened.

This pathetic human who wreaked so much havoc on so many people and who thought he was some kind of tough guy, couldn't even kill himself in the end. He couldn't make the police do it for him either, although they could have had they chosen to be executioners rather than police officers that morning.

The fire finally took total hold of the house, and of those media watching the smoke from Taranna, most assumed that Bryant had or would perish in the inferno, and probably thought that would have been the best outcome for all. I know that I assumed this mass murderer had had his fifteen minutes of fame, or infamy, and would soon be dead.

But no – the man who inflicted so much pain on others had no threshold for pain himself.

When the heat from the fire inside the house finally got too much and the back of his clothes caught fire, he rushed out the door – not armed with his semi-automatic weapon and blazing away in some death or glory exit from this world, but with a tiny handgun which threatened no one and gave no one an excuse to fire on him.

The surrender was swift and a whimpering Bryant was taken into custody, suffering fairly serious burns to his back and buttocks, but the injuries were not life threatening and he was immediately treated at the scene. I heard later that one of the officers involved in the arrest of the naked Martin Bryant had commented that the gunman could be seen to be armed with a 'very small calibre weapon'.

The ultimate irony from all this was the fact that the paramedics (Stride and Allen) who accompanied and treated Bryant on the drive from Taranna back to hospital in Hobart, were the paramedics who were first into Port Arthur the previous day and who did what they could for those that Bryant had not managed to kill during his murderous spree.

While they say simply, "it was just another job", the dedication and professionalism of this pair in the immediate aftermath of Port Arthur was a wonderful example for all who aspire to such a profession.

To have seen the extent of death and injury inflicted by this man only twenty hours earlier and to then have to treat and accompany him to hospital, and be civil to him as well, I think was above and beyond the call of duty.

Several Special Operations Group officers did have ample opportunity that morning to shoot Martin Bryant. They didn't, because as one explained to me, they are not executioners.

They had no reason to fire because they were not under threat and neither was anyone else. Many readers will be thinking that had they pulled the trigger that morning, no one in the world would have minded, and they may be right.

But consider what would have happened six months or so down the track.

I believe that given the current attitude of the media, which has developed in recent years, we would have seen some investigative television or radio program asking the question, "Why was this man executed? Why was this social misfit killed? Why was a man armed only with a pistol gunned down by automatic weapons?" And so on and so on and so on.

Those working for such programs would have already forgotten about the thirty-five dead people.

There is no doubt that such a program would have been made and indeed there are a very few people who are still now prepared to peddle the nonsense that Bryant was a patsy from some greater international campaign to disarm the world.

In this area, I believe the media has an undue influence

on people who have to make what are at times history making decisions. I don't say that some people should be above observation or scrutiny, but has the media at times become far too intrusive for the good of the community?

Bob Fielding and Barry Bennett deserve the highest praise for their efforts at the Port Arthur Forward Command Post. They did an exceptional job and I feel proud to have been part of their team.

Port Arthur has been one of the most traumatic occurrences in my life but it is comforting to know that if such incidents ever happened again in this State, Tasmania Police have proved they can handle any situation.

With Seascape burnt to the ground and Bryant arrested and taken off to hospital, the police were preparing for what was one of the most important aspects of the entire Port Arthur incident. As macabre as it sounds, the media was to be taken through the site and shown the scene of the killings.

The media is voracious in its need for information, and, for television, they need pictures. Our problem was to decide how best to get them this information and those pictures without having mayhem in what was still a major crime scene.

There had been some discussion during the Sunday night about who was in control at Port Arthur – was it the Coroner who was investigating the deaths or was it the police because it was a crime scene. After the discussion, I think it was decided (to the chagrin of some that night), that although no one had yet been arrested it was indeed, a crime scene; and that police officers needed to be in charge to do their work for any prosecutions that would follow.

Superintendent Jack Johnston was the man in charge of the crime scene at Port Arthur. He was also responsible in great measure for the success of this innovative idea of bringing the media in to see what happened, for themselves.

He organised for the bodies, except those in the Broad Arrow Cafe, to be removed from where Bryant had left them and to have the areas covered with blankets. But nothing could cover all the blood, and so the horror of the events was real enough for the media to see, and, in turn, portray to the world.

Of course the media was not shown inside the Broad Arrow Cafe. That was an area kept off limits to them that Monday morning. Not because of any censorship, but simply because there was not time enough to finalise the police investigative work and remove the bodies before the media arrived.

The sights in that cafe were best left unseen by any general public. Twenty people died within that small area in a very short time from gunshots from a high powered semi-automatic weapon built specifically to kill and maim people during wars and armed conflicts.

Whatever you, as a reader, are imagining it looked like in the cafe that morning, I am here to tell you it was worse than anything you can contemplate. It was eerie. It was silent. It was dreadful.

Adrian and I made the trip from Taranna to the Historic Site early, to talk to Jack, and go through what he wanted to do with the media that morning. Again, having him in charge of this particular operation showed Tasmania Police in a good light to the world. We left soon after, confident that all was under control.

But back at Taranna we nearly had another revolution on our hands.

The media had heard about the bus trip being organised into the site, but because they had not gone from Taranna back to Hobart for the 7 am briefing earlier, they would not be included. It was, they believed, some form of punishment for them.

The fact was a bus had been organised for the tour, but in Hobart apparently there had been a serious miscalculation in the numbers of media at Taranna. There were a few calls made again, and it didn't take long to have authorisation for a second bus to be chartered. But, while that was a simple decision, it took time to get hold of the bus.

Anyway, the media had to cool their heels at Taranna with no new developments between about 9 am and midday when the buses finally arrived.

The Forward Command Post was being dismantled and the Special Operations Group was withdrawing to Hobart. The intelligence section also pulled out quietly. In fact, just as quickly as everything arrived at Taranna the previous afternoon, it left again.

With the clean up, the pictures of Bryant which had been used by Bennett and Fielding during the operation were thrown into a cardboard box. I thought little of them until the next day when a picture of Bryant appeared on the front page of the Mercury newspaper. Happily however, I can say the picture was not stolen from those at Taranna. All the ones we had were still in the cardboard box.

Richard McCreadie, who later became Police Commissioner, published the results of his investigation into how the newspaper obtained their picture, and it does nothing for the credibility of the journalists involved, because the picture was stolen from within Bryant's house in Hobart.

Again, I would point to what used to be the journalists' code of ethics as it relates to the obtaining of material and information, and say no more.

While the media waited for the buses to arrive; they prepared their gear for the tour – there seemed to be a kind of excitement in the air as if they were going on some historic excursion, which I suppose they were. But it would be unlike anything else any of them had ever experienced.

At midday the buses arrived and took on those at Taranna who wanted to go and see what had happened at Port Arthur. No one stayed behind.

The first stop was Seascape, the beginning and end of the killings. It was still smouldering, and police investigators were at work sifting through the rubble.

They were then taken further down towards Port Arthur, past the Fox and Hounds Hotel, where Linda White had gone for assistance after being shot and seriously wounded while driving past Seascape the day before – that was just as Bryant had arrived back at the holiday cottages after creating mayhem and murder. She was another of those who were in the wrong place at the wrong time that day.

From there it was on to the service station where a young woman had been murdered in her car and her friend kidnapped and taken by Bryant to Seascape; and to the toll booth at the Historic Site where four people had died; and not much further on to the site where a mother and her two small children died;

and then past the Broad Arrow cafe to the section of the car park where the buses park – and the scene of another four deaths.

During the trip the media was strangely quiet, there was some attempt at bravado, but now Port Arthur was real to those who until now had only regarded it as a good story.

The blood in the cars and on the roadway was real. They were looking at the sites where people, not 24 hours earlier, had been hideously murdered. This was not Hollywood, nor was it an exercise. This was the site of the worst mass murder in Australian history, and it had happened at a tourist attraction in Tasmania.

Superintendent Johnston explained the sequence of events as best as he could to the media that day, and did so with firm authority. Only once did someone attempt to do the wrong thing. They were cut down immediately by Jack with a simple sarcasm laden comment, "And I thought I had asked you all so nicely to do the right thing."

After two hours the buses returned to Taranna and let those who needed to pick up their cars and gear get off and make their own way back to Hobart. The looks on the faces said it all. Gone was any levity that was evident when the buses arrived. Instead, there was a sombreness that can only be obtained by visiting a hell, such as Port Arthur was that day.

Soon the media had all gone. The police had gone. The Telecom technicians were taking out the extra phone lines they had worked so hard the previous night to install, and John Hamilton was left to put his reception centre for the Tasmanian Devil Park back into some sense of order.

Strangely enough, at the height of all this activity, some tourists arrived to visit the Park. I guess they were on holiday and simply kept to their schedule and may have been totally unaware of the use to which the Park facilities had been put in the previous twenty-two hours.

With no more to do, I also left Taranna and headed home. Only then did I realise I had been there for 24 hours, had had no sleep and had been involved to a large degree, in probably the biggest news story in recent Australian history. But I would have rather worked on something that was just as historic but less murderous.

I called the office when the mobile phone came into coverage range on the way back from Port Arthur and said that I wouldn't be in that day, I would go straight home and sleep. There was no argument, nor was any expected, it had been a very tough twenty-four hours.

I include here, just one of the newspaper stories that the people of Tasmania, Australia, and indeed the world, woke up to that Monday 29th, April.

From the *Herald Sun* newspaper, and headed: "Woman Runs For Her Life As Bullets Fly". It reflects the media frenzy for information during that Sunday afternoon and evening.

They had managed to get some early quotes from some people in the Port Arthur area and were trying to piece together the whole story.

"He left the site shooting as he went, shooting everybody he could see," said Wendy Scurr, who was working at the front desk of the historic site.

Mrs Scurr phoned for help and then ran for her life when the gunman began shooting. The man had been chatting to people 'quite lucidly' when he went into the cafe and started shooting 'many many' people indiscriminately, including children, staff, locals and tourists.

"He continued shooting when he left the site," Mrs Scurr told the satellite TV service.

"He was in a car at that stage, he's on foot now," she said.

She said she phoned for help and "ran for my life along with hundreds of other people at the site". Outside the cafe he continued shooting at tourists as they screamed and tried to run from him.

"He wasn't going 'bang, bang, bang' – it was 'bang' and then he'd pick someone else and line them up and shoot them," witness Phillip Milburn said.

"It was a gun that was meant to kill people."

He also shot at a number of cars and later shot more people dead at the nearby Fox and Hounds Hotel. "There is a lady dead in a car at the top of our drive," cafe owner Phillip Kelly said.

"When he holed up in a house after driving about five kilometres from the original shooting site, he began firing at the helicopters taking his victims to hospital, another witness said. The Royal Hobart Hospital was put on full disaster alert and more than 200 police were sent to the area".

Thirty-five people lost their lives at Port Arthur that weekend, twelve from Tasmania, twelve from Victoria, one from Western Australia, six from New South Wales, two from South Australia and two from Malaysia. Seventeen were male and eighteen were female, with ages ranging from 3 to 72 years.

A later assessment of the situation by ambulance officers was that the fatal injuries were predominantly high calibre gunshot wounds to the head, chest or both, mostly at close range. The critical injuries were all gunshot wounds to the upper body; and other injuries included gunshot wounds to the limbs and legs and penetrating fragment injuries.

The Ambulance report said that due to the calibre of the weapons used the result was a high number of early fatal injuries. It has not escaped the Ambulance Service that had lower calibre firearms been used the ratio of dead to injured would probably have been reversed with the probability of more live patients with critical head and chest injuries. In fact, treating ambulance personnel were convinced for some time that Bryant had been using a shotgun in the Cafe due to the significant number of 'peppering' wounds they noted. This turned out to be bony fragments from other victims. The power of the weapons was such that one bullet fired at a car pierced the metal pillar between the driver and passenger windows, killed a woman, and exited through the other side of the vehicle.

There was one barely reported feature of Port Arthur in which Tasmania was in fact leading the rest of Australia in coping with a disaster of this magnitude. After the relevant police investigations, Hobart's Government Contractor, Ray Charlton, who provides mortuary ambulance services was called in to help transport the bodies to Hobart.

He had two vehicles, an ex-Tasmanian Ambulance Service Ford F-100, capable of carrying four bodies; and a Chevrolet truck, to the chassis of which he had attached a refrigerated covered compartment capable of storing sixteen bodies.

The vehicle was considered by some as an expensive aberration that would never have a use. In fact I know Mr Charlton had received a degree of denigrating criticism from some sectors of the community about his vehicle and his job.

So, contrast that uninformed criticism with what the Coroner from Port Arthur, Mr Ian Matterson had to say sometime later;

> "At Port Arthur it (the sixteen capacity unit) was a highly prized possession. One cannot overlook that the road between Port Arthur and Hobart is narrow, undulating and about 100 kilometres long.
>
> "In just two return trips the Chevrolet carried the majority of the disaster victims to the mortuary, a task that otherwise would have required eight return trips by conventional mortuary ambulance. Mr Charlton's foresight became a lesson in efficiency," Mr Matterson wrote.
>
> He also went further; "The foresight of our mortuary ambulance contractor in providing a vehicle of more than average size for the purpose of removing the bodies from a disaster site was of utmost importance in the overall efficiency in clearing the scene.
>
> "I would recommend that every other State give consideration to liaising with Mr Charlton to ensure they have the information necessary to have similar efficiency."

TUESDAY 30TH APRIL, 1996
And the Rest of the Week

Tuesday saw the mayhem continuing. People throughout the country were still trying to come to terms with what had happened and why it had happened in Tasmania.

On another front there was ethical outrage within the local media ranks over the *Mercury* newspaper publishing a front page picture of Bryant under the heading, 'This is the Man', before he had even been charged by police.

The outrage was mostly from the competing newspapers locally who also had pictures of Bryant from Monday, but did not print the full facial shots of him because of the law of contempt. They had managed to get pictures of Bryant as he was being taken into the hospital.

The *Mercury*, a *News Limited* paper, apparently took the line that they had the picture, and, probably, that Rupert Murdoch had more money than the State of Tasmania to fight legal battles, and so they would publish and be damned.

Well, damned they were by their opponents, but no doubt congratulated by Rupert, because sale of that particular (stolen) picture, no doubt made News Corporation a lot of money around the world.

Despite all sorts of threats and investigations, the Director of Public Prosecutions in Tasmania has not prosecuted for contempt. It leaves open the question whether the law is actually worthwhile or enforceable, or needs changing. Certainly the incident demands a clarification of what is legally right and wrong.

Two years later, in April, 1998, the then Police Commissioner, Mr Richard McCreadie in a submission to the Senate Select Committee on Information Technologies, gave his account on how the photo had been obtained.

His submission alleged that a newspaper team (from the Mercury) had distracted a lone police officer guarding Martin Bryant's home the night of the Port Arthur shootings while a reporter entered and stole a photograph of the gunman.

He told the Committee that evidence of the alleged scheme was supplied by a Hobart Mercury employee, who informed on reporters and a photographer. The Committee, ironically, was reviewing self regulation in the information and communications industries and Mr McCreadie's submission was reported only by the Mercury's competitor, the *Advocate* (Sat, April 18, 1998).

Mr McCreadie said that after police were swamped by complaints about how the *Mercury* was able to publish the photo, and with suggestions, obviously, of favoured treatment, a review of photographs proved the published image had not been taken into police possession.

"A confidential telephone call from a person who identified himself as an employee of the *Mercury*, alleged the manner in which the photograph of Bryant had been obtained," he told the committee.

The Commissioner said the informant indicated that while a journalist and a photographer engaged the police guard in conversation, another journalist broke into Bryant's house and stole the photograph.

"The detailed description of the house in the newspaper report that went with the photograph could only have come from someone who had been inside," he said.

Mr McCreadie also told the committee of the media's behaviour during April 28, describing the scene at Port Arthur near the exclusion zone as "frenzied and the competitiveness between themselves as ugly".

He cited the instance of a photographer who became friendly with locals and then broke the police cordon by going through dense bush towards the site of the Seascape cottages.

"Here was a gunman in a cottage with hundreds of rounds of high powered ammunition and absolutely no regard for human life. The photographer was not only placing himself at risk but those police who had to find him. At the best this could only be described as foolhardy, and at the worst, as stupid. The photographer became lost in the bush and stumbled out onto the road hours later, to be found by police," he said.

Mr McCreadie said the purpose of his submission was to provide the Committee with an insight into the role of the media in a major incident.

Tasmania was traumatised by the killings. There was a need for strong leadership to enable the State to not only recover but move forward.

Step up newly elected Premier, Tony Rundle.

Rundle had only been elected just five weeks earlier, and to add to his problems, he was leading a minority Liberal Government. The new Parliament sat on the afternoon of 30th April. Because of the events at the weekend, it was a ceremonial sitting only, and the House would rise on its adjournment that day until the next week.

It was the Premier, Mr Rundle who spoke first, and moved;

"That this House resolves to express its condolences to the families, relatives and friends of those who lost their lives in the tragic events at Port Arthur on Sunday, 28th April; its sympathy to those who were injured or otherwise involved; and its thanks to all those who assisted in dealing with this tragedy.

"There is no sense or reason in what happened at Port Arthur on Sunday. It is beyond the comprehension of any of us. On a sunny, Sunday afternoon when families were picnicking on the tranquil lawns at Port Arthur a tragedy struck. We do not know what motivated it – we may never know – but within one hour thirty-two men, women and children lay dead; three more were to die later at the Seascape cottages. Nineteen people were also injured and everyone at the Historic Site and everyone in Tasmania was scarred by these terrible events.

"Port Arthur, a place with a long history of sorrow, grief and anguish, had added another chapter to its bloodied and tear stained past. There is no one in this State who has not been moved by what has happened. You can see the grief on

the faces of our people on the streets and in the shops, and in a small closely-knit community like Tasmania, the pain is that much more intense because it is that much more closely shared.

"Not all of those who died came from Tasmania; some were from interstate and some from overseas but to the members of this House and to all Tasmanians that makes no difference. We mourn for all of them and all our thoughts are with the families and relatives and friends of all of them. Our sympathy is with the injured and we wish them all a speedy recovery.

"Our thoughts are also with all of those other people involved – the staff at Port Arthur, those who live or work at Port Arthur, many of whom sheltered and comforted those at the scene; those who were visitors to the Historic Site on that dreadful day; all the ambulance personnel; the police and the State Emergency Service personnel; the helicopter pilots, volunteers and others who had to deal with the carnage. Many of those people are only young themselves, far younger than most of us in this House, and they dealt with scenes and realities that would shock any of us to the core.

"This morning I met with many of the ambulance officers and paramedics who were the first on the scene. Along with Mrs Milne, I also visited some of the injured at the Royal Hobart Hospital and expressed on behalf of all Tasmanians our sympathy and concern. Of course we also thank the doctors, the nurses, the hospital workers who cared for the wounded and the counsellors who are working with the community to heal the other wounds.

"Mr Speaker, when this motion is passed this House will be adjourning for a week as mark of respect. Tomorrow morning at 10.30 there will be a State service at St. David's Cathedral. At a later date a special memorial service, organised by a committee chaired by the mayor of the Tasman Municipality, will be held on the Peninsula. Around Tasmania this week flags are being flown at half mast and tomorrow as a mark of respect Tasmanians will stop at half past ten for a one minute silence. These are the outward and public demonstrations of our mourning but the private grieving and the sense of community shock and anguish will go on for much longer.

"For these events to have any meaning our little island must draw strength and resolve from its despair but that of course is for the future. Today is for the dead and injured and those who helped them, and for all of us to reflect and to mourn. I therefore commend the motion to the House."

Next to speak was Mr Michael Field, the Leader of the Labor Opposition;

"Mr Speaker, I stand in support of this motion.

"Like many people, when I first heard of the tragedy at Port Arthur I did not believe it; this sort of thing did not happen in Tasmania. Like many people I immediately rang my family to find out what was going on and to reassure myself that those I loved had not been involved. By the time I got back to Hobart on Sunday evening the death of thirty-two innocent people had been confirmed. I still could not believe it, it was too unreal. My colleagues and I met to discuss what had happened. There were tears, sheer disbelief, confusion and total and utter sadness as we tried to come to grips as a group with the news coming from Port Arthur. This tragedy had happened in our State, our home, to people that we had known or passed in the street just the day before.

"During the past 48 hours there has been a feeling of total emptiness as we try to go about our ordinary tasks. The nature of the tragic events at Port Arthur has made our daily actions seem trivial, inconsequential, and even pointless. My colleagues and I have discussed the tragedy endlessly to try and find some meaning to what has happened but the answers are just not there.

"Expressions of condolence and sympathy just do not seem enough. As the story of the tragedy unfolds the horror of what happened to those innocent victims only makes us grieve more as we try to comprehend the terror that must have gripped those caught up in the massacre.

"It has been a tragedy that has touched a nation. We grieve now as a nation for those who have lost their lives. We feel nothing but compassion for those who lie injured in the Royal Hobart Hospital, the friends and families of those involved, police officers, ambulance officers and others who had to witness the aftermath and somehow go on about the job they have been trained for.

"We grieve for the loss of our innocence, both as a State and a nation, where this sort of tragedy is not supposed to happen. As Tasmanians we grieve for the attack on our *quality of life, our most treasured possession and something which we have proudly proclaimed to the rest of the world, a world that is now looking at us, judging us and shaking its head in collective disbelief.*

"Now is the time for the Tasmanian community to join as one, to unite in our grieving and show the rest of the world that we will recover no matter how long it takes. We must not look for instant retribution. As a community we have to address the daily impact of violence on our lives. We have a moral duty to do as much as we can to take violence out of our lives. Now is the time to look further than just the obvious to find out why it happened and to do everything in our power to ensure that it is never repeated.

"We now must try to decide what has to be done to ensure those who died are not forgotten. We must try to learn the lesson of their tragedy. We have to ensure that the people of the Tasman Peninsula in particular are given every possible means of support. These and other issues will dominate public debate in Tasmania for a long time to come. The Port Arthur massacre will be with us as long as we live.

"There is much more I could say but now is not the time. For now I think it is important to commend the Government and to especially commend our police and emergency service personnel for their actions, which have been above and beyond the call of duty.

"Finally, on behalf of my colleagues I express my deepest sympathy for all those people who have been directly touched by this tragedy and pledge our total support to whatever actions are taken to support the families of those involved."

The only other person to speak that day was Green Independents leader, Christine Milne; *"Mr Speaker, on behalf of the Tasmanian Greens I rise to support this motion. We are all in shock and disbelief – thirty-four people are confirmed dead and more are wounded; some are known to us others are not, and the whole of the Tasmanian community is now moving as if in slow motion. There is a quiet in the streets and our usual capacity to act, to work, to lead, to speak, is impaired as we try to overcome the numbness and come to terms with the enormity of the horror and confusion which has befallen us.*

"As I lay in bed last night trying to think what to say that could even have any impact, any expression of what I was feeling, I was aware that right across the State other people were also lying awake; people feeling insecure, people feeling frightened for the future of Tasmania; people despairing; people angry; people praying for some insight; people crying and others just staring. And my mind was filled with the images which will come to symbolise this tragedy, not only for all of us but for the world: the father who lost his whole family; the child dying in her mother's arms; the people sitting at the tables with cameras and bags just having lunch, suddenly confronting death; the small rectangle of dry sticks beneath the tree where the small girl's body fell; the old couples who had begun to do what they had always planned to do when they retired; the women pushed under the tables by their husbands; the young man who threw himself in front of his wife and three-month old baby; the Camp Quality puppeteers; the woman who yelled

the warnings; the tourists including a seven month pregnant lady, huddled in a cottage on the site not knowing whether the gunman would burst through the door at any moment. And the reason that these images are so powerful is that they convey a picture of all of us: ordinary people doing ordinary things. They could have been our children, our parents, our friends, our aunts, uncles, husbands, next-door neighbours.

"In the context of Tasmania, in a population of 475,000 people, 'Each victim is myself'. And as their stories emerge and we share them we all know that, 'There but for the grace of God, go I'. We used to think Tasmania was removed from the atrocities of the rest of the world but so too did the people of Dunblane. As one British headline said, 'Where on earth is safe?' Mr Speaker, it has to be here. If we are to recover as a community from the evil that has occurred here we cannot be frightened of legislative action.

"We have watched the emergency services – the police – men and women – the medical teams of doctors, nurses, counsellors, and support staff, do their jobs with incredible compassion, dedication and commitment and we are deeply grateful. We have watched the generosity of spirit in the community, both on the Tasman Peninsula, throughout Tasmania and throughout Australia, as people offer spiritual and practical support and reach out to each other. Now, as legislators, we must do the same. As a community we are all in this together. As Tasmanians, the greatest expression of condolence and sympathy we can offer to the families and friends of those who have died or have been wounded is to ensure that their suffering and death has not been in

vain. We must resolve by our collective action to rebuild our community, to make it more cohesive, more caring and more secure so that something good can come out of this disaster – something which may bring some peace and comfort to those who are now enduring such terrible suffering and agony and to whom our hearts reach out. Mr Speaker, the Tasmanian Greens support the motion."

The Speaker then asked all honourable members to indicate their support for this motion by standing in their places and observing one minute's silence. The House then adjourned.

But Tuesday, 30th April, also saw a lot of backroom work with Canberra over the Memorial Service to be held in Hobart the next day.

The Prime Minister, Mr Howard, wanted to attend the church service at St David's Cathedral in Hobart, but because of Parliament sitting and the logistics involved, did not think he had the time to visit the site at Port Arthur itself.

Politically this would have been very unwise and his office was told this in very plain words. But the answer was 'no', there was no time to attend both the church and Port Arthur. No amount of counselling of the Prime Minister's advisers could sway that decision throughout the day and in fact it wasn't until late on the Tuesday night that things changed.

I think in the end the fact that Canberra was told that the best local advice would be that the Prime Minister should not come to Tasmania at all if he wasn't going to also visit Port Arthur as well, did get through.

Because of regulations, the Prime Minister is not permitted

to fly in single engine helicopters or planes and this was one of the major problems the organisers faced that night. However, once this was overcome things got back on track and the trip was on, albeit a brief one. The details were still being finalised at 11 pm that night.

While all this was going on, that same Tuesday night we had the Premier go to the lawns outside the Royal Hobart Hospital to appear live on CNN with John Raedler, their Australian correspondent. I knew John from when we worked together at 2GB many years before. The appearance by Tony Rundle that night was one of his best television performances ever, under very trying and difficult circumstances.

I also renewed acquaintances with Steve Leibmann that night. He had come down from Sydney on the Monday to broadcast the national *Today* program from Hobart for the week in the wake of Port Arthur.

There was a kind of unreal atmosphere outside the hospital that night. The lawn was covered with television gear from all the mainland networks and some overseas crews; and not 100 yards away was Bryant, under guard in a Hospital ward and being treated for burns. Fifty yards in the other direction was the main Hobart Police Centre.

The general consensus amongst those media crews working that week was an incredulous, "how did this happen in Tasmania?" But it did.

Prime Minister Howard, Opposition Leader Kim Beazley, and Australian Democrats Leader, Cheryl Kernot, all made the trip to Port Arthur on the Wednesday morning with local politicians, Tony Rundle (Premier), Michael Field (Opposition

Leader) and Christine Milne (Green Independents).

I had to go back to the site early that morning to organise the media again – to ensure they got adequate coverage of what happened but also to help shield some of the locals from unwanted intrusions on their enormous private grief.

The day was crisp and clear and eerily silent when I arrived shortly after 7 am. There were few people at the site at this stage. The Broad Arrow Cafe was still bedecked in floral tributes and the windows had been blacked out to prevent people seeing what was inside.

The twenty bodies had been removed by this time, but inside the restaurant was still a chamber of horrors.

The format of the day was to be very informal – with the Prime Minister and Premier to meet and talk with some of the staff of the Historic Site and other locals who may turn up on the day.

By the time the official party arrived by helicopter, a reasonable crowd of locals had turned up and gathered in the car park outside the visitors centre. They were milling around, still obviously in shock and trying to comfort each other, but the grief was tangible, even to outsiders.

In my role as media liaison officer, I went and spoke to the locals, and felt that because I had been through the Sunday night I had some affinity with them. That is not to say however, that I had any of the experiences that some of these staff from the site had on the Sunday afternoon, and they were hurting badly still on this Wednesday morning.

The media probably never understood that many of the local people at Port Arthur took an instant dislike to them from about the Monday morning after the murders. There was much angst about the front page pictures of local chemist, Walter Mikac's murdered wife and two children for a start, and it went downhill from there.

Many people do not understand what the media considers to be its job – the papers thought that telling of Walter's loss was conveying the horror of Port Arthur, and they probably were. But to many people on the Peninsula who read the paper on that Monday morning, they took it as an outrage against Walter and indeed their entire community.

The relationship between some on the Peninsula and the media has never been mended and probably never will be – and in large measure it is based on the flawed concept in the mind of the public about what the media is and what it should or should not do.

There is also, I must say, a lack of understanding, on many occasions from the media, on just how affected some people were by Port Arthur.

But on the Wednesday morning, there were some who were upset that the media was there to cover the visit by the Prime Minister at all, and in fact wanted them removed from the site.

I told them that this was impractical if not impossible and that the media was there to do a job and would do it, but that I would talk to them and try to minimise what they (the Port Arthur people) thought would be most harmful to them.

This I thought was a reasonable compromise and I tried hard to make it work to the satisfaction of everyone involved.

Some of the locals that day were a complete mess and I knew that they were going to get even worse as they approached the

Broad Arrow Cafe to place flowers on the steps.

Remember, some of these people had seen and worked in some pretty horrendous conditions only two days previously and had not been back to the scene of the massacre.

Howard was at his statesmanlike best that day – I know people either love or hate him, but to me he has always been at his best when he speaks off the top of his head about something he has genuine feelings about.

His words to those at Port Arthur that day were what the nation was trying to express but had difficulty in doing so. It was not a day for political point scoring and there was obvious unity from all political groups that morning. In some ways it is sad that it takes a national tragedy of this nature for politicians to realise that politics is not the centre of the universe for most people.

The media were allocated a roped off position near the Broad Arrow Cafe. This gave them good coverage of the arrival of the official party and the laying of floral tributes on the steps of the Cafe, without being intrusive and being able to put cameras up the noses of people and asking them the inevitable question, 'how do you feel?'

How do they think people who have been through what they had would feel? I think the 'how do you feel' question is one of the greatest cop outs in the media today.

All went well enough until a couple of Historic Site staff went to put their tributes on the steps. These people were in terrible shock and were grief stricken to the point of hardly being able to walk. It was a truly tragic sight for anyone to see and I did my best to let the crews get their shots as these people approached the cafe steps and then for a few seconds as they placed their flowers.

Then I quietly asked the camera crews to 'click off' or at least not concentrate on these particular people. In fact I explained that they had not even wanted the media to be there in the first place and that in good faith I had brokered a deal which I hoped would suit everyone.

All crews were glad to be able to 'click off' except one – a mainland network which has two numbers in its call sign and it was not SBS. The reporter for this network had made a proper nuisance (for want of a better word) of himself on the Peninsula on the Tuesday and was continuing to do so on Wednesday by insisting his cameraman keep shooting.

Now my aim during all the Port Arthur stuff had been to ensure that, where possible, everyone had everything they needed – that way everyone is happy – but this guy was going on like some prize clown.

I stepped in front of his camera to block the view and that sent him over the top.

Apparently he had recently returned from assignment in Uganda or Angola or somewhere else in Africa where there had been a civil war; and where he said he had seen all sorts or carnage and mayhem, and he apparently thought that his experiences justified him in doing exactly what he wanted to.

But if that was the case I would have thought he should have been more attuned to what was happening that day in Port Arthur than anybody else, but he wasn't. As I kept standing in front of his camera he kept insisting that he had a right to shoot and I had no right to prevent him; and that I was an idiot, and that I didn't know what I was doing, and then he came up with the claim that I was trying to censor the news.

Through his tirade he apparently never heard a word I had said. By then, I had had enough. It had been a long Sunday/Monday. Tuesday had been little better and I wasn't in the mood at 8 am on the Wednesday to put up with this sort of behaviour which I thought was way out of line.

I told him there were two ways he could continue to cover the event for his network. My way, which involved him being part of the media pack and behaving in a way which would not harm his industry; or his way, which involved my having the police officer standing next to me arresting him and his cameraman and removing them from the Port Arthur site.

This seemed to set him off even more – but then a wonderful thing happened. The other cameramen, both television and newspapers working at the site that day turned on him – and told him to shut up and behave himself because he was "giving us all a bad name".

This was realisation by the great bulk of the media who had been involved since the Sunday night, that there indeed needed to be some sensitivity in the coverage of this story; and for that I was eternally grateful. Anyway, the upshot was that his cameraman did click off.

The rest of the visit that morning went off almost without a hitch. As is always the case when Prime Ministers or Premiers or heads of state visit anywhere, there is a tentative itinerary or program worked out in advance outlining what they will or won't do, and this day we had advance word that the Prime Minister would not be speaking to the media at Port Arthur.

I duly conveyed this to the media in good faith; but as often happens the plans were changed suddenly at the site, and he did speak to the media and without warning.

There was an unseemly rush by the crews to get their cameras and microphones to where the Prime Minister was standing with a small group of Port Arthur survivors. He had obviously and shrewdly judged the climate of the day better than anyone else, and chose to speak about his feelings on the tragedy.

He was marvellously eloquent under the circumstances and I think he sowed the seeds there and then for uniform national gun laws in Australia.

But already at this stage, the Wednesday after the Sunday, there was growing angst between many of the locals who were at Port Arthur on the day of the massacre, and the media, and it got worse as time went on. Understandably to most, many were still in shock on the Wednesday and didn't want to talk to the media but the media was insisting on new angles each day to 'keep the story alive'.

As a journalist (by then of nearly thirty years standing) I understood the need to have new leads on stories each day, to take them that little bit further, but when those who played a key role on the Sunday did not want to tell their stories (yet), some of the media resorted to underhanded tactics.

Having said that, I should now record an instance where I believe the media were wrong in the Port Arthur coverage – not all media, just one reporter and he knows who he is. And by wrong I mean non-thinking in relation to the impact particular lines of questioning can have on people. There is no harm in asking hard questions, but they can be asked in an appropriate and proper and polite manner whatever the circumstances, and I think there is now far too much 'go for the throat' approach without considering ramifications.

Typically, I have found this comes from media who fly into Tasmania to cover a story and then fly out again, but I guess it is not unique to Tasmania. All I would ask them is, would they ask the same questions in the same way if they had to live in that place after the incident, be it a massacre or an election or some other event.

In most cases the answer is no, because they don't have to stay there after the event. They are beastly careless as to what upset and harm they cause while they are covering the story. They also forget what harm their actions do to the reputation of the media in each of these places that they come to and trample over sensitivities and ethics.

In Tasmania over the last decade, we have suffered greatly at the hands of the media who fly in to do some story or other and then fly out again leaving behind mayhem and resentment.

The State is an easy target for such tactics, and I am not being paranoid in making this claim. I have seen it happen too often. It seems many in the media find it easy to come here to do a story on the Port Arthur massacre, forestry, mining, gay rights or some other issue; and to present half a story or an ill-balanced report, or a story that makes Tasmanians look particularly, and, mostly unfairly, silly; and then fly out again until the next time.

Anyway, on the Tuesday after the Sunday massacre this particular reporter managed somehow to get a list of names of Port Arthur historic site staff who had been involved on the Sunday afternoon and was telephoning around to interview them, but with some he wasn't being entirely honest in his approach.

For instance, there was a staff member in the toll booth who saw Bryant armed with a gun, coming up the road from the cafe. Unaware of exactly what had been happening minutes earlier she promptly thought he was coming to rob her of the day's takings, so naturally enough, hid herself in the back storeroom of the booth and locked the door.

Bryant arrived at the booth seconds after shooting dead a mother and two children and then killed another four people whom he dragged from a parked car at the toll booth gates, took their car and left the site to continue his killings.

By any accounts this would have been an horrendous experience for the staff member hiding in the booth. To hear the shots and probably even the voice of the killer and his victims before the gunfire, would you not be wondering if he was going to break into the booth and kill you too? Of course you would, and of course, you would have terrible thoughts for a long time after such an experience.

This woman however, got a phone call barely 48 hours after this particular incident in which a man identifying himself as a reporter for a particular network, asked her "why she hid in the toll booth while four of her friends were killed by Bryant just outside". This was outrageous and I believe a deliberate and wilful distortion, aimed at getting the response he did.

He was told that was not what happened, and so he then said "well I am prepared to give you the opportunity to set the record straight just come and do an interview with me".

And this woman, mortified to think that he was broadcasting the fact that she "hid while her friends died" (and she did not even know the four people killed at the toll booth), agreed to talk to him on camera, although she had already indicated to everyone that she was not ready to talk about what she saw and heard.

But put in this position by the reporter, what alternative did she have? Wasn't there a media gun just as dangerous as Martin Bryant's weapon pointed at her head? Talk about media intimidation!

Did this reporter not understand the ramifications of shock, or the desire of some people to not yet relive the horror they had been through? Was he only interested in getting some poor person on television in a very distressed state to talk again about Port Arthur?

This tactic has become all too common place these days, and I don't think it does the industry reputation any good at all. But thankfully the woman mentioned this approach to someone and they got her off the Peninsula for the rest of the day and kept her from the media until she was ready to speak.

But why should anyone be put through this added type of trauma. Did he think that the honest approach in asking her if she wanted to tell what she saw/heard/knew about events that Sunday would not work? Did he think that she should be bludgeoned into talking to him, for fear that he was doing an adverse story on her anyhow.

But there is a God – I know. I complained to his editors about his action and I would expect that others also did, and that reporter was, soon after Port Arthur, taken off the road, and for a while, was not an on the road reporter for the network. However, as time passed, I notice he was again back on the road.

What price do network editors pay for insensitivity?

I believe this is an area the media needs to look at itself, for self-regulation. No one can make them accountable so maybe they should make themselves accountable, because there needs to be accountability to ensure this behaviour doesn't continue to be endemic in the media.

After the memorial Church Service at St. David's Cathedral in Hobart on that Wednesday morning, there was a group of Port Arthur staff who decided they would talk to the media.

Sue Hobbs was the public relations officer for the site, and was actually the first person to tell the world about the killings. She was onsite within minutes of the shootings and took most of the early phone calls from the media. I think the first call was from CNN (America's Cable News Network) and she spent much of the afternoon while the phone lines were open, giving her account of the massacre live to a worldwide audience. CNN would have picked up the story from their local affiliates and wire services in Australia.

But on the Wednesday, Sue came into my office in the Executive Building in Hobart and said that half a dozen staff wanted to talk to the media. Just this once, because they realised the need for stories and also to keep the media off their backs and the backs of many others who still feel they couldn't talk. I thought it was a good idea and should help fill any void the media was finding in getting new angles.

But what a harrowing news conference it turned out to be with Wendy Scurr telling of putting tea towels in the back of people's heads where they had suffered huge bullet injuries and of trying to help those still alive. Wendy was a trained volunteer ambulance officer, and she did what she could for the wounded that day but the incident has had an enormous personal impact on her.

The local *Hobart Mercury* newspaper had coverage of the news conference in their 2nd May edition, with a story written by Jodi DeCesare.

> "Wendy Scurr yesterday told of her terror as tourists and staff were hunted like rabbits during Sunday's massacre at Port Arthur. The tour guide at the Port Arthur Historic Site was among four staff who risked their lives to save others.
>
> "Distraught and shaking, the four yesterday choked back tears as they detailed their horrific hours at the scene, both during and after the massacre. Two of them, Ian Kingston and Paul Cooper, entered the Broad Arrow Cafe while the gunman was still inside in a desperate bid to help. Three of their workmates died in the massacre.
>
> "Devastated by what they saw, they described how they tended to gaping wounds, doing the best they could with tea towels and basic first aid kits. People died in their arms. But perhaps their most difficult task is still to come – coping with the grief and coming to grips with the sickening scenes.
>
> "Wendy Scurr, a trained ambulance officer, was the first person to notify police that a gunman was inside the Broad Arrow Cafe. She was in the information office only metres from the cafe when she heard what sounded like a gas explosion in the restaurant. Then somebody came out and said, 'He's killing everybody ... run,' she said.
>
> "Instead, she phoned for help. 'I was a little bit distressed as to whether they believed me; that was a worry. I told them there was slaughter going on; that people were being killed

everywhere. I said for God's sake get as much help here as you can. They wanted a contact number, I said I won't be here!'

"With two others, Mrs Scurr fled the information office – 'it was glass fronted and we had nowhere to hide' and headed for bushland behind the cafe before the sound of gunshots grew weaker. 'That was the most frightening time of all; not knowing whether that man was going to come back. We were so vulnerable. We felt like rabbits at a hunt,' she said.

"Then she ran into the cafe to help victims, to be faced with a scene of absolute devastation. The people with her had relatives inside. 'They were deceased,' she said. 'There was very little I could do. There were people in there who had lost families; they were very brave, they helped me ... I can't talk about the scene. Only three people were alive.'

"In the half hour before the local ambulance arrived, Mrs Scurr grabbed first aid kits and started to treat the wounded with the help of two surgeons on holiday. 'I didn't think. I just went about what I had to do. I found other people outside that I could help.' (One was Brigid Cook, who was in charge of the cafe who went back in to get her staff out and was shot in the leg). 'I used tea towels as padding. There was very little you could do for the injuries these people had except keep airways open and stop bleeding.' Three people treated by Mrs Scurr inside the cafe survived.

"Paul Cooper, a tour guide, was walking towards the Broad Arrow for lunch when the shooting began. 'I heard lots of shots,' Mr Cooper said. 'I knew what it was and men ran out and said there were people killed.' He too grabbed a *first aid kit and ran into the cafe, while the gunman was still inside. 'I couldn't do much at all. I just went around and tried to find people who were alive. That was really hard to do. I heard more shots and I thought about dying then so I rushed back out with my first aid box.' He herded tourists from the scene and locked them inside another building.*

"'Then I was on my own with a first aid box, with a hat on, and I thought "geez" I'm gone here. I was looking for cover. I went towards trees, ducking and diving through the trees. I yelled at people to get in and lock the doors and get down.' He then went back inside the cafe. 'Some people died in my arms. I ran out to the bus then because I realised I had not checked the bus. A man was there, he was still alive, his wife was holding him. All I could do was pack his wounds. Down the back of the bus there were more people gone. I went to help a woman down the back but she died also. It was a matter of trying to find people that were not so badly hurt; most people were gone.

"'I don't think you could class it as heroics. At the time it's something you have to do. You just forget about what's going on, a few short seconds you think about dying and then you just keep going.'

"Ian Kingston, the Site's security officer, was directing traffic at the car park beside the cafe when he heard loud banging.

"'I was totally unaware of what was going on inside,' he said. 'I ran to the front door, entered the cafe and once I saw what was going on inside I immediately left and started to co-ordinate evacuation of people. What had happened inside

had happened; my concern was to make sure we protected as many people outside as possible.'

"He said he thought he may be shot. *The thought crossed my mind but I was only one of 500 people; we needed to get the site cleared. It didn't hit me until about midnight as to what the consequences could have been,'* he said.

"Peter Burke, the Historic Site's commercial operations manager and responsible for the Broad Arrow Cafe was heading to the East Coast on a work conference with other staff when the incident occurred. *'We were told there had been a disaster. It was just unbelievable. We got about half way back to Port Arthur; we couldn't find any information. That was making everybody pretty jittery because some people with us had loved ones on the site and didn't know who, what, where or why. That was traumatic.'*

"When they arrived at Port Arthur, their worst fears were realised; relatives were among the dead. *'It was fairly eerie; to me it looked like a scene from MASH with helicopters and ambulances going every which way, people being carted left right and centre. There didn't seem to be panic. There was urgency but no panic, everybody was doing something. A calm came over the place until later in the evening when we heard there was a scare out, that they thought he (Bryant) may have got loose. It was pretty terrifying later in the evening. I had to ferry some people out and three shots went off. We were thinking has he (Bryant) made a run for it? What's he done? That put pressure on everybody again. I am still numb about the whole thing. It was something that you never want to see again.'"*

That news conference, in the Hobart Town Hall, in a room which was too small to really accommodate all the media who turned up, certainly gave the world, if not the media, a new perspective on just what had happened and how horrific the events were. It also gave some indication about heroic deeds on the day.

And then the conference was over. The almost shell shocked media were told that after this conference by the Port Arthur staff, there would be no more with any of them until further notice. That is, until they (the staff) felt more able to speak about the events again.

This they seemed to accept and I did my best in the next six or seven months to shield these particular people from the media spotlight, because I had not heard or been told they were yet ready to speak again. This was always my clear understanding of what they wanted to happen.

Unfortunately, later in the year during the recovery phase of this outrage several of these same Port Arthur staff accused the Government (and indirectly me) of not letting them have their say about Port Arthur; of not letting the media talk to them; of shielding them from the media, when my clear understanding was that this was what they wanted.

I was in touch all that year with Port Arthur and the Peninsula people and not once was I told, by them or anyone else, that these people were again ready to speak to the media and so, I, in good faith, kept telling the media, when they asked, that there had been no change in their preparedness to talk.

And like many stories, after time, the media stopped asking.

When I got home that night (Wednesday) there was a letter

from Jack Newman, written from Risdon Prison on Sunday night – in part it read – "I am watching television and see that someone has murdered at least twenty people at Port Arthur. How can he live with himself? I have to live with the fact I killed one person and I don't know how he can live with himself. I hope he dies".

The local community at Port Arthur arranged to hold their own memorial service on site on the Friday – and the unease with the media got worse as the week went on.

The organising committee decided that the media could attend, but only if they stayed away from the actual service, and stood in the middle of the oval outside the old penitentiary; and did not film towards the roofless, historic church where the service was being held.

I told them this was a ridiculous proposition, and that either they invited the media to attend and made proper arrangements for them to cover the service; or decided that it would be a closed event without the media. But either way they had to make it clear what they wanted.

The Police and Emergency Services people had made arrangements for a bus to take the media to the service, and a few days earlier had asked for those interested to register as a way of booking seats. Not many had registered and I remember calling those that had and asking them if they really wanted to go to the service. Surprisingly, while the Port Arthur people thought the media could not get enough of the event, by the Friday the media could handle no more. They didn't really want to go to what was going to be a huge outpouring of personal grief.

And so when I put out a fax through my office saying the people of Port Arthur had requested the media not to attend the service, there was collective relief from most that they wouldn't be forced to go.

They had also had enough grief in the last week. They were also suffering shock if not near exhaustion from what had been a week from hell; if not a hell of a week of reporting.

But then, there is always one, isn't there?

The grapevine from Port Arthur did detect one photographer from the mainland who was staying near the site that week and was happily telling all and sundry that he was going to sneak into the service on the Friday and take pictures, despite what anyone else wanted to do in regards to having it as a closed ceremony, with no media.

Once identified, his editor in Sydney was contacted and the situation explained to him. Assurances were given that even should this person infiltrate the area and take pictures he, the editor, would personally ensure they would not be used. I don't know if the cameraman did show up that day, but if he did, the editor was as good as his word. Just shows there is more than one way to catch a monkey.

The Friday service was held in the old church on site, and was packed by locals and site staff. I was one of the few outsiders there, and my task was really just to check that the media weren't there, as they had undertaken not to be.

It was an emotional and moving service with a lone piper playing from the hill behind the ruins and there were lots of tears during and after the proceedings. It was something the Peninsula people needed to get their grieving process properly underway.

And it wasn't only staff and family and relatives and local community leaders who cried – the minister who conducted the service was also an emotional wreck by the end of it. These were not easy times for such a small and close knit community.

Just before the start of the service I met, for the first time, John and Sue Burgess. I knew their teenage daughter, Nicole, had died in the Broad Arrow Cafe, and developed an immediate affinity with them.

They have stoically suffered through an unquantifiable loss, yet were a source of strength that day to others who also suffered. The card Sue left on the steps of the Cafe was poignant – reading in part "you were the one who kept me organised, who will organise me now?" Anyone with a daughter of similar age to Nicole and obviously of similar characteristics could not help but be moved, and I was. Indeed, my daughter Sarah had told me that her school class had been due to visit Port Arthur on an excursion on the same Sunday that Bryant unleashed his murderous rampage. One has images of 'sliding doors'.

I admire the way John and Sue have handled their loss in the last few years; but for a time refrained from establishing a close friendship with them probably because of some guilt feeling that I still have my teenage daughter, they don't. And I can only imagine the suffering they are enduring.

I also ran into John Hamilton and his wife (from the Tasmanian Devil Park) and they introduced me to many other locals who were involved in the outrage of the previous Sunday.

Having worked at the Forward Command Post and been back again on Wednesday for the Prime Minister's visit, helped me at the Hobart media conference on the Wednesday afternoon to liaise with the survivors and also the organisers of the Friday service. I felt I was as involved in Port Arthur as anyone else, and was to be, until Bryant was finally sentenced to die in prison.

Personally I found the service hugely emotionally draining, and must admit that on the way back to Hobart that afternoon, just past the Seascape guesthouse, I remember seeing a small red car which had crashed off the road. I was about the third car to arrive at the scene. People were already on their way to check on the occupants; I couldn't handle any more and so kept driving.

There was a ceremony in Hobart on Sunday, 5th May, to publicly recognise some of those who provided assistance immediately after the shootings just a week earlier.

The *Mercury* newspaper carried this report in its 6th May edition.

> "*Wendy Scurr, the woman who raised the alarm at Port Arthur last Sunday, still looked shaken by what she had seen as she collected a certificate for outstanding service yesterday. Memories of last Sunday were fresh and tension was still in the air, visible when the crowd jumped at the sudden sound of a popped balloon.*
>
> "*Mrs Scurr, a Port Arthur guide, was the first volunteer ambulance officer to receive a certificate of commendation from the Governor of Tasmania, Sir Guy Green, in front of 200 dignitaries including ambulance officers and their families at Tasmanian Ambulance Service headquarters in Hobart.*
>
> "*She returned to her seat to be comforted by fellow volunteer ambulance officers Robyn and Colin Dell of Taranna. 'We didn't do this to get an award, we did what we were trained to do,' Mrs Dell, a nursing sister, said later.*

She thanked ambulance officer Noel Dalwood, who had trained the Tasman Volunteer Unit for the last 15 years. 'The training definitely helped,' she said. 'Without it we would have been going nowhere.'

"Among those who received certificates of commendation for outstanding service were Tasman Volunteer ambulance officers, Gary Alexander and Kaye Fox, doctors Pamela and Stephen Ireland, the Dells, Tim McKinlay, Ruth Noye and Lesley Kurek, Dunalley volunteers Roger Garth, Jodi Branch and Jim Giffard, Helicopter Resources, the Tasman and Dunalley volunteer ambulance units, Tasmanian Ambulance Communications and all the emergency services.

"Before he presented the awards, Sir Guy Green said the demands on voluntary ambulance service officers had been enormous. They had carried a disproportionate amount of the shock of the tragedy.

"'Of the nineteen people injured at Port Arthur, all have survived,' he said.

"'You have made an important contribution to how soon we'll come through this. Ambulance officers have to serve people every day of the year and do it without fuss and fanfare and sometimes without adequate recognition.' Sir Guy said he wanted to acknowledge their work and their dedication to duty."

All this time Bryant was still in hospital being treated for burns; and he had now also been charged with murder. Police made their first attempt at interviewing Bryant on the night of 29th April.

At about 6.30 pm, Detective Inspector John Warren, the officer in charge of the CIB within the Eastern Police District, unsuccessfully tried to interview this person in his room at the Royal Hobart Hospital. At the time they arrived Bryant was sedated, and so Inspector Warren would return the next day.

Bryant's response to the allegation that he was responsible for the shooting at Port Arthur was that he didn't know anything about it, and he had been a long way from Port Arthur, surfing.

"I've been unjustly accused," Bryant said.

He declined to participate in a video recorded interview and Inspector Warren then formally arrested him for the murder of Kate Elizabeth Scott. (She was one of the thirty-five victims of his obscene behaviour).

On 6th May, 1996, the Port Arthur Taskforce was established under overall command of Superintendent Jack Johnston with Detective Inspectors John Warren and Ross Paine maintaining control of the ongoing investigation.

While Bryant was in hospital anonymous bomb threats were being made and staff received death threats for treating the gunman. The situation in Hobart became generally unpleasant.

Feelings in some areas were running very high. There were calls for the return of the death penalty and all sorts of graffiti was painted on hospital walls.

By the Sunday (5th May) it was decided Bryant was well enough and would be better off in Risdon Prison hospital, and so he was transferred there in the middle of the afternoon, ironically at about the same time just a week earlier, he had gone to ground at Seascape after his terror at Port Arthur.

Much to the chagrin of some in the media, the transfer was

made with little fanfare and no publicity. That was why I got hostile phone calls later in the afternoon demanding to know why they weren't told the transfer was being made.

Some even suggested that it was deliberately organised to coincide with the Governor presenting awards to ambulance officers who attended Port Arthur. I think the media at this stage was seeing too many conspiracy theories for their own good.

The facts were that Bryant was being threatened; the hospital staff were being threatened; and the daily working of the Royal Hobart Hospital was being upset by repeated bomb threats. So where would you have put Bryant?

The obvious answer is the maximum security prison hospital, and that was what was done. As for not telling the media, so they could photograph the transfer, in fact all they would have got was a picture of a van under escort going from the hospital to the prison. That is what security is all about and not everything is a media event.

Imagine if there had been a staged transfer especially for the media, and that somehow a 'nutter' managed to infiltrate the event and kill Bryant, a la Jack Ruby and Lee Harvey Oswald!

In America they are still battling conspiracy theories over the killing of John Kennedy. We would have had the same problem here if someone had managed to top Bryant before he went to trial. And besides, I for one would not have wanted to try to handle the media conference that would have been held to explain that Bryant was killed by a 'nutter' during an event staged for the media.

Any kindly officer who may have agreed to such a staging and then lost an alleged (at that stage) criminal of Bryant's notoriety would very soon have the media at his throat accusing him of incompetence.

So unfortunately for the media, some things are simply not possible, if only out of a sense of self preservation in case things go disastrously wrong – but where the media can be helped, they generally are.

THE RECOVERY PROCESS

With Bryant now in jail, all sorts of programs were being put in place on the Tasman Peninsula to help those affected by the massacre.

Later on there would be criticism that not enough was done for more people and that the area was neglected. All I can say to that is from what I saw neither the Peninsula nor the people were neglected. I know, from the Government viewpoint, the amount of effort and resources that were put into the area immediately after and for a long time to follow.

For the management of the Port Arthur Historic Site, it was an absolute nightmare. There was not, and still isn't, a handbook to tell anybody or organisation how to handle an incident where thirty-five people are murdered at a worksite; and management got themselves into a lot of trouble through no real fault of their own.

For instance, within days of the shootings they put out a newsletter to all their staff and in it apparently said something along the lines of "our staff reacted in the manner we would have expected".

Now most reasonable people would have taken this as a compliment, or at least I would have thought they would. But some on the Peninsula took it as an insult.

Those individuals believed that their actions on the Sunday did not receive proper recognition in that particular newsletter, and this became a source of angst into the future.

Have no doubt, there are a number of people who experienced Port Arthur who will never be the same again – and that is not an accusation but rather a reality. But I also think that they have been affected to the point that they misconstrued a lot of things that were being done for the people of Port Arthur, and took on a bunker mentality very early on in the recovery.

A couple of weeks after the shootings, I was invited to a de-briefing session, along with Darcy Tronson. We duly arrived at an office to be met by what I believe to have been an army psychologist. He asked how we felt about the entire incident.

Darcy was able to say he was fine. I said that I was also fine, but then for some reason the psychologist asked what had had the most impact on me. In hindsight I would have much preferred the 'de-briefing' to have been an individual thing. I felt uncomfortable talking in front of Darcy, who was my boss.

Anyway, it just poured out. I burst into tears while recounting the fact that what had most impacted on me was the female radio reporter who insisted at every news conference on the night of the shootings, on asking "how many children had been killed". To this day I think the question was insensitive and unnecessary at that time. But she insisted on doing it every hour.

I then said no more about the incident and we ended the de-briefing. Such events these days would be called counselling.

By 9th May, the Government had put in place the Port Arthur Tragedy Recovery State Management Plan which drew together the efforts of all State Government agencies, in support of the measures being taken by the Tasman Peninsula community through the Tasman Council Task Force and the response in other parts of the State.

In announcing the Plan, the Premier, Tony Rundle, said the task of the community recovery is an enormous one and much of the load would be carried by community and business groups, schools, the churches and a host of other organisations outside Government. He went on to say he wanted to ensure the State Government agencies were in a position to help and support the activities of those groups.

The problems faced by the Tasman Peninsula area were huge.

More than 80 per cent of employment in the region was directly related to tourism. Before Bryant's rampage, tourism was estimated to be worth about $9 million a year to the region, attracting more than 200,000 visitors annually.

On 10th May, 1996, just ten days after the tragedy, all caravan parks, cabins and other forms of group accommodations were reporting almost zero occupancy. All casual staff had been told to stay at home and group bookings as far out as August had been cancelled. All tourist attractions and restaurants were already proposing to open on weekends only, until there was evidence of a pick-up in business.

Clearly, the area was hurting badly with people staying away. Not I think through any lack of support, but because they simply didn't know if they were wanted, or would be welcomed, or indeed what to say to people when they got there. It was a huge problem and it called for quick action if the area was not to suffer total economic collapse.

At the same time, the Prime Minister, true to his word, moved quickly on changing Australia's firearms laws. Fortuitously, the Australasian Police Minister's Council held a special Firearms Meeting in Canberra on 10th May, 1996.

The resolutions from that meeting, agreed to by a Premier's Conference in June, formed the National Firearms Agreement. It resulted in restricted legal possession of automatic and semi automatic firearms and further restricted the legal importation of non military centre fire self-loading firearms to those with the maximum capacity of five rounds. The agreement also committed all States and Territories to a firearms registration scheme and licensing of people in order to legally possess and use firearms. Previously, only handguns needed to be registered; rules around long arm registration varied between States and Territories. It also saw the introduction of laws designed to minimise the legal acquisition of firearms by unsuitable persons.

The Agreement was implemented by the States and Territories over the next couple of years, including a 12 month national amnesty and buyback scheme allowing gun owners to sell newly banned firearms to the federal government so they could be destroyed.

The National Firearms Buyback program saw something in the region of 650,000 firearms handed in by members of the public. The cost of the buyback was paid for by an addition to the Medicare levy on all taxpayers which was to raise $500 million.

Meanwhile, Premier Tony Rundle decided action needed to be taken to bolster the flagging Port Arthur economy, and

In Memoriam

Winifred Aplin
Walter Bennett
Nicole Burgess
Sou Leng Chung
Elva Gaylard
Zoe Hall
Elizabeth Howard
Mary Howard
Mervyn Howard
Ronald Jary
Tony Kistan
Dennis Lever

Sarah Loughton
David Martin
Noelene Martin
Pauline Masters
Alannah Mikac
Madeline Mikac
Nanette Mikac
Andrew Mills
Peter Nash
Gwenda Neander
William Xeeng Ng
Anthony Nightingale

Mary Nixon
Glenn Pears
Russell Pollard
Janette Quin
Helene Salzman
Robert Salzman
Kate Scott
Kevin Sharp
Raymond Sharp
Royce Thompson
Jason Winter

over and comfort the children with quiet words of reassurance and a personal invitation to look after them if or when they decided they might visit the Historic Site for themselves. I don't know to this day if they have ever visited Port Arthur, the site of their parents' murder, but I am sure if they haven't the invitation from Neil still stands.

From Ballarat it was back to Melbourne for a flight to Canberra and more media interviews and another flight to Sydney for that night.

The John Laws radio program was the most widely listened to in Australia, and Laws was very generous and gracious in the time he allocated Rundle. The pair in fact struck an instant rapport and at the end of the interview Laws actually offered the use of his voice, free of charge, for any new advertising that Tasmania may do in the future to help rebuild tourism in the wake of Port Arthur.

The fact that the most recognised voice in Australian radio and television was never used by Tasmania in any campaign after Port Arthur was indicative of the muddled headed thinking that was going on in some areas. I certainly would have thought that the use of John Laws' voice in any radio advertising campaign would have been well worthwhile. The offer certainly shows him in a different light to the cash for comment saga which embroiled him a few years later.

From Sydney it was on to Brisbane where there was a touching moment at the State Special School at the Royal Children's Hospital within the Royal Brisbane Hospital. The kids had taken up their own collection for Port Arthur and presented it to Rundle at a small ceremony in the hospital.

Here were kids who were not at all well, in fact seriously ill, thinking about the kids on the Tasman Peninsula and they were besides themselves with excitement that the Premier himself had come to visit them. It was Michael Arlidge, Carlos Watson-Ferriera and Chantelle Robson, who so ably made the presentation to Mr Rundle on behalf of their fellow students.

But by now there was a new mood taking over in parts of Australia. For the previous three days the publicity and round of interviews had been positive in that they focussed on Port Arthur and what people could do to help those in the area, but now the gun debate was starting to take off.

The television interview in Brisbane with one of the current affairs shows dropped the Port Arthur people like a hot potato that night.

The producers kept the Premier waiting for more than an hour at the studios while they 'got ready', and they assured him that they wanted to do their bit for Port Arthur and the people of the Peninsula. But when it came time for the interview, it was an ambush over gun laws – very little about Rundle's real mission that week.

He handled it well enough, although I always feel an ambush is a fairly cynical way to interview someone. I found you often get far better answers when the 'talent' has some idea of what is coming, but there is a fixation now within television especially about trying to shock the 'victim' with some revelation, accusation or claim. The 'gotcha' type style which so many of the public know and hate.

Inevitably however, the whole mission was about to come off the rails, because of the argument about uniform national gun laws being pushed by Prime Minister John Howard, and the debate about some guns being banned altogether.

An early flight on the Friday morning took us to Adelaide, via Sydney, where there was a surprisingly good reception from the media, given that the mission had been going all week. In fact the *Advertiser* had carried an editorial on the Wednesday in which they said "one of the discoveries Tasmanians have made in the time of trial is that they have a good premier in Mr Tony Rundle".

Remember, that Rundle had become Premier of a minority Government in Tasmania just five weeks before Port Arthur, and so it was literally a baptism of fire for him. I must say the event also upset any political agenda of his own that he may have had for those early days of his Premiership.

Port Arthur and its aftermath dominated Tasmania for about the next 12 months and I think a lot of Rundle's plans for Government were unavoidably sidetracked. I can remember one day sitting in his office in Hobart and remarking that he had personally handled the entire situation pretty well. He was probably only half joking when he replied that he didn't really want to go down in Tasmanian history only as "the Premier for Port Arthur".

Government is never easy. Minority Government is extremely difficult and minority Government with a Port Arthur hanging over your head is well, nigh impossible. The goodwill mission ended that Sunday, May 19th, back at Port Arthur with an Ecumenical Memorial Service at the Historic Site.

Again another emotional and moving service; and again I was there to help with the media on the day. I didn't have a lot to do with the organisation of the service this time because I was away for the week with the Premier on the goodwill mission on the mainland. The Site had organised for consultants to put together some plans and media kits for the day and there was only one hitch.

The media kit contained all sorts of material including a request to photographers to find an unobtrusive position before the start of the service, and to remain in that position for the duration. Not a difficult task I would have thought; and it wasn't for all but one from a weekly tabloid magazine.

This character simply walked onto the site late and started to head in among the congregation. As he went past me I whispered that he had better get a shot quickly and then get back to where the other photographers are, or else I would have a riot on my hands.

He politely told me to go and do something to myself that is anatomically impossible, because he was going to do what he liked. The policeman who was with me, who was also aware of the media arrangements for the day, heard the exchange and beckoned the cameraman towards him.

Just as politely he told the snapper what the rules were for the day and if he didn't want to follow them he could leave the site, with or without a police escort; but he (the policeman) said he hoped this person would not cause a scene at a memorial service.

And he didn't – he simply disappeared to the back of the crowd and joined the other cameramen. I know it is a fiddly point, but one person doing the wrong thing makes it hard for media liaison officers and the police, who don't like having to be seen to monster the media. At most times we are doing our best to help them.

This Sunday was also the day the nation first saw the memorial cross which had been erected on the waterfront at the Historic Site. It was supposedly a temporary placement but I doubt now that anyone will move it. It has taken on a sort of sacred persona and has become a pilgrimage place for many who visit Port Arthur. (Eventually it was moved nearer the Broad Arrow Cafe in the newly built memorial gardens).

It was also the day of Neil Noye's inspired address in which with a trembling voice he spoke about "our mates not letting us down in our time of need".

As Mayor of Tasman Council he knew more than most the amount of goodwill and aid and assistance that flowed into the area in the wake of the killings. He also knew more than most the problems that would be facing the Tasman Peninsula in the rebuilding that was to come.

Neil's speech that day contained a lot of, and said a lot about the man.

"On April 28 our small community was dealt a fearful blow, and we wondered if life could ever be blacker. We had never thought our beautiful Peninsula would be the scene for such an horrific crime against humanity.

"Our confidence in the old solid values of life, held by people of goodwill everywhere, was badly shaken. How could we ever recover, we asked ourselves. While I never doubted recovery was possible, I looked to the hurdles we faced with some alarm. But today, less than a month on, we gather here as a community bound together by a common belief in the

collective goodness of humanity.

"It's a belief that's been restored by the overwhelming goodwill shown to our community by fellow Australians and countless people overseas. In common Australian terms, our mates have not let us down. They have come forward with a deeply moving generosity of spirit to help us along the tough road to recovery. We could have asked for no more.

"I have lived on the Peninsula for a long time, but never have I been so proud of my community as in the past weeks. It has shown resilience beyond expectation and a cooperative spirit which causes great hope for the future.

"Port Arthur will remain a deep scar, but I have no doubt it and the rest of the Tasman Peninsula will overcome this terrible chapter in its history. The list of those deserving of the community's deepest thanks is too lengthy to detail here.

"From the pre-school kids and their painstakingly written notes of condolence, to our own State Government which has pulled out all stops to help us, there are many to whom we are grateful.

"I hope the cruel acts committed here, so recently, will not turn people away or destroy Port Arthur, which is such a significant landmark in our nation's history. Rather, I hope that with time as the hurt fades, as it inevitably will, the association of lost friends and loved ones with this place will make it dearer to us. Perhaps we can honour them best by cherishing life more and by not wasting a minute with mean spirited thought or unkind deeds.

"And finally I say to the friends and relatives of the

victims, yours is the heaviest sorrow, but we share the burden as much as we are able".

The service ended with the release of thirty-five pigeons from cages at the foot of the Huon Pine cross, and symbolically they circled up from the cross and did a circuit of the oval on which the congregation was gathered and then, as the sunlight broke through the clouds, they flew from the site.

As the local Mayor, on the Tuesday after the shooting, Neil had visited all the local people who had lost loved ones. He knew eight of the people who had been killed, and he knew Bryant. He had met the gunman sometime earlier when he went to Neil's property wanting to buy calves for the Bryant farm at Copping.

Neil Noye also attended many of the funerals of those killed, both in Tasmania and interstate, describing them as very traumatic experiences.

In his address to the six thousand people gathered there that day, the Premier Tony Rundle told them that "there was no sense or reason for the wickedness that had occurred three weeks before. Yet even on that blackest day there were great shafts of light. Wickedness passes, but courage, strength in adversity and hope for the future are with us forever. In just twelve weeks the daffodils will bloom, and blossom will burst forth from the trees".

State Cabinet met the next day (20th May) at the Fox and Hounds Hotel complex not far from the Historic Site in an effort to show the people of the Peninsula that they had not been forgotten and that they would be helped.

And not only were there problems for the people most

closely associated with the massacre. Think about the prison authorities who had just been handed responsibility for the care and wellbeing of a person who killed thirty-five others without a thought.

The prison officers were left in the unenviable spot of having to protect Bryant and keep him away from the threat of harm from other inmates. He was remanded in custody after a bedside court hearing in the hospital and within a week was admitted to the hospital wing of Risdon Prison.

He was kept in isolation and under suicide watch at all times in the early days and his very presence at the prison put a strain on already stretched resources.

And then there was the question of his court appearances later, how would they be handled and what special arrangements would have to be made.

As it happened, the Department of Justice had for some time been working towards the introduction of a system enabling prisoners on remand to appear before the Courts through video links from the prison.

In fact, provision was made in the newly constructed court building in Liverpool Street in Hobart for such a facility, and Bryant was the ideal inmate on which to make use of it. He was due to appear on 22nd May, and everyone including the Chief Magistrate was of the opinion that it would be desirable to arrange for the appearance to be by video link because of the obvious security implications involved in bringing him to the Court and back to the prison.

Another fact in favour of a video link appearance was that Bryant was still suffering from burns and his medical condition would mean special attention was needed for any court appearance with the likelihood that he would still be unable to walk at the time of the scheduled appearance.

There was also another issue the legal people had to consider. That was the question about whether there needed to be an amendment to the Justices Act which refers to a person being 'brought before' justices. Advice was sought and received and there was no impediment to a video link appearance.

But arranging media coverage for this appearance also presented problems. While Bryant wasn't actually in the court the Chief Magistrate, bearing in mind the controversy still raging over the *Mercury's* earlier decision to print a photo of Bryant before he was charged, was keen not to have more pictures taken of him.

To this end, it was the Chief Magistrate himself who decreed that the media were welcome to watch the video link hearing, but without cameras. This was a very specific and very clear edict.

On the day, all cameras were left outside the courtroom during the appearance and it wasn't until it was over that the problem with one Agency photographer emerged.

Because the appearance was brief, barely minutes, the sketch artists who had flocked to the hearing had no time to do justice to any drawing of a likeness, and so asked the court officials if they could have the tape re-run and paused so they could prepare sketches.

There was no problem with having this done, in order to assist the media as much as possible, but the Hong Kong based photographer from *AFP*, the French newsagency, by this time had brought his camera back into the courtroom where the video machine was being used.

For some reason he took a shot of the screen, and when challenged, brushed off concerns by saying that the light was not sufficient to get a shot anyway, and "of course he wouldn't go against the Chief Magistrate's orders in relation to pictures". Personally, had I been there I think I would have had the court officials confiscate the film and consider contempt charges. But I wasn't.

Anyway, you wouldn't be surprised to learn that indeed the picture did turn out pretty well and yes it was printed far and wide around the world. All of which just serves to provide you with the background as to why *AFP* found it so difficult to get much cooperation when they turned up in Hobart later that year to cover the real story, the trial of Martin Bryant.

By now the gun control debate was raging across the country with protests by firearm owners who felt they were being victimised, and similar protests by anti-firearm groups who wanted all guns banned.

The Prime Minister stood his ground and at the Premier's Conference in Canberra early in June, which I attended with Premier Rundle, he had all states sign up to the National Firearms Agreement. That is not to say all Premiers simply walked in and meekly signed. It is my understanding that there was an amount of strident debate and even a Federal ultimatum, before final agreement was reached.

Mr Howard was totally convinced about his push to reform gun control in Australia, but now admits that the biggest mistake he ever made during the entire debate, was to wear a flak jacket, or body armour, to a gun rally at Sale in Victoria on 16th June,

1996.

His staff tipped off the media to the fact he was wearing it, and the pictures of it bulging across his back went world-wide. I can understand if he was advised by security staff to wear it, but my understanding is that they didn't.

As always, Mr Howard was a brilliant orator on his feet, be the crowd friendly or hostile. The crowd in Sale was one which probably was less than friendly. But he took to the stage and delivered a defence of what he had done.

> "Last night I saw on national television, Mr Ted Drane, the National President of the shooters' organisations in Australia – And he said something with which I totally agree. He said that he was and his fellow shooters were not criminals, they were Australians. And I want to start my address to you today by saying at no stage in the weeks that have gone by since the decision taken by the Federal Government and the Police Ministers in that decision, at no stage have I sought to describe or categorise the attitude of people who enjoy shooting or people who are shooters as being in anyway criminal or un-Australian. I have not used language which has sought to label or smear you or other tens of thousands of law abiding citizens.
>
> "I acknowledge and I have acknowledged in the very beginning and I do so again today, that the decisions that have been taken by all the Governments in Australia, decisions that were confirmed last Friday at the Premier's Conference meeting, they are decisions that will inconvenience, they will influence the activities of people who hitherto have engaged

in law abiding pursuits. And at no stage is it the basis of the decision taken by the Federal Government and at no stage is it part of my own personal attitude that in any way any of you or any people who have been involved in what are, up until now, the lawful possession of firearms, in no way have you people been involved in criminal behaviour at any stage. And that is not the basis for the decision. But the basis of the decision ladies and gentlemen is that we believe that it is in the national interest that there be a dramatic reduction in the number of automatic and semi automatic weapons in the Australian community.

"In taking that decision I recognise and my colleagues recognise that many people who previously have been carrying on a lawful pursuit are going to be inconvenienced. I know that, I regret that, I apologise for that but that is the basis of our decision. And it has been taken, ladies and gentlemen, because we believe not just because of those tragic events at Port Arthur, they were the culmination of a long series of events in this country which have demonstrated as has been demonstrated in other parts of the world, that there is a clear link between the volume of powerful weapons in the community and the extent to which they are used in an indiscriminate manner.

"If you look at these statistics out of countries such as the United States, if you compare them with statistics in other parts of the world there is an irrefutable link. And in taking the decisions that we have taken we are mindful that they will impact unevenly on sections of the community.

"I am mindful that people who have never owned a

weapon, have never had any desire to own a weapon are not going to be affected in the way in which people such as you are being affected. I know that, I regret that and that is a matter of concern and apology to me but it cannot alter the responsibility of a national Government to take a decision that it believes serves the greater good of the entire Australian community. And that my fellow Australians is the basis of the decision that we have taken. We have not sought in taking this decision to brand any of you people as being anti-social. We have not sought in taking this decision to brand people who enjoy shooting as being engaged in any kind of criminal activity and you will find that nothing that I have said and you will find nothing that I will say in the future that will in any way take that attitude.

"But there come occasions for any Government to take decisions which can only be effectively implemented in the interests of the overall national good if they involve some disproportionate inconvenience and some disproportionate deprivation for one section of the community. I'm sorry about that but there is no other way that we can achieve the objectives. And it is always, my friends it is always the responsibility of a national Government to weigh up the gains and to set them against the losses. And the gains to the Australian community of there being fewer weapons of great destruction in the community, in my view and the view of all governments throughout Australia very, very significant indeed and that is why we have taken the decision.

"Now I don't pretend for a moment ladies and gentlemen that the decision that we have taken is going to guarantee *that in the future there won't be other mass murders. I don't pretend that for a moment. What I do argue to you my friends is that it will significantly reduce the likelihood of those occurring in the future. I wouldn't be so foolish as to say that it is going to completely eliminate them. And I know that in the wake of what happened at Port Arthur that people have argued that one of the greatest weaknesses in the present system, and one of the causes of mass murder is that we have an approach to mental health laws that are too permissive."*

There was more to the speech and then Mr Howard took questions from the crowd, but for the purposes of this work what I have included outlines the 'whys' behind the Government decision clearly enough.

I do not want to indulge in a firearms law debate in this work and it matters not if one agrees with the Prime Minister's stand or not, the fact is that since Port Arthur there have been no similar atrocities in Australia.

But I know law abiding firearm owners across the nation still resent the fact the Mr Howard, on whoever's advice, wore body armour on that day, whilst at the same time referring to the crowd as friends, and fellow Australians.

THE TRIAL OF MARTIN BRYANT

Those not closely involved can have no idea of the enormous amount of work that went into preparing for the trial of Martin Bryant on charges of murdering thirty-five people at Port Arthur in Tasmania.

The State's Director of Public Prosecutions, Mr Damian Bugg, worked with all the witnesses and indeed wrote to them in August to answer their questions about what would happen during the trial.

He told them that not all people spoken to by the police would be called as witnesses, and that of the many hundreds involved in the case, he expected only a fraction would be required to actually attend court.

Bugg, aware of the impact the massacre had had on the Peninsula was pushing to get a trial before the end of the year (1996). He told the witnesses that if any had to attend the court they would be provided with an opportunity to discuss or be briefed on their evidence.

"We obviously cannot 'coach' you (witnesses) in what evidence you give, but we can fully explain the procedures, the evidence you are being called to give and so on" Bugg wrote.

Some witnesses were also concerned about security, and Mr Bugg undertook to have discussions with the Chief Justice to ensure that appropriate steps were taken to protect witnesses from any pressure or threat.

"Where requested I will attempt to provide protected access to the Court building if witnesses wish to avoid public and media attention outside the building" he went on.

So as you can see, the people likely to be most involved in a trial were very nervous about both the public and the media, and not only Mr Bugg, but I, had to operate in this climate while at the same time trying to assist the media do their job.

I think a lot of the problems ahead were caused by the 'public and those affected by Port Arthur', not fully understanding what the role and the job of the media really is, or appreciating the fact that Port Arthur was indeed big news on a world wide scale.

Having been involved with the media management at Port Arthur and being Press Secretary to the Premier, I was also somewhat targeted by some individuals affected by the event, who were trying to get their message through to the Government, via me.

It was an invidious position in which to be placed, but I did what I could under difficult circumstances to ensure that their grievances and problems were addressed. Many were; some apparently weren't; and some could not be addressed, for whatever reason.

I did attend a particularly depressing meeting in mid October where about a dozen staff/relatives from the Port Arthur site vented their anger on myself, Gerald Jones (a former temporary

General Manager of the Site, and a member of Environment Minister John Cleary's staff) and Michael Langley (Board Member of Historic Site Management Authority).

The meeting was initiated by the husband of one of the staff, and the basis of it was that unless something was done to help these particular people very quickly there would "be more deaths from Port Arthur". The assertion was just left hanging there. What do we do about this situation?

Both Gerald and I had had long meetings with this man before, and we were concerned about what he was telling us; and we tried to put in place appropriate support systems. I also had meetings with this man and Greens leader Christine Milne.

However, we were all the time aware that we may be being used as a back door way for some people to 'get back' at the Historic Site management for real or perceived shortcomings on April 28th and since.

It was real tightrope stuff, but with someone suggesting that people are about to kill themselves or others if you personally don't do something about it, there was no option but to try to deal with their issues.

I never want to be in that position again, but I have a clear conscience that I did what I could at the level at which I was operating at the time. Much of the night dealt with the experiences of those who were on site on 28th April, and some felt there was a lack of recognition for their efforts; that they were all heroes; and that all those on duty that day deserved medals.

Others spoke about problems and confusion over pay entitlements and legal advice and entitlements for the cost of burying their loved ones after the massacre. Still others spoke of the fear, suicide and death threats which had been made against them and the ongoing problems of being on medication.

A great deal of anger was directed at an appearance on television a couple of days earlier by Mike Langley when he was alleged to have said something to the effect of "life was getting back to normal at the Site".

He had not seen the clip nor had any memory of saying such words, but that was how it was interpreted by these particular people and they were savage in their attack on him because of it.

They spoke of people (them I guess) wanting to smash the television set when they heard the comment, or of "how dare he say that". These people were badly affected by Port Arthur, no one denies that for a moment, but I believe they were also not seeing the greater picture at the time.

Everyone I was working with was very careful not to offend or upset anyone, particularly this group of people with which we had been dealing since shortly after the shootings. All were consciously avoiding talking in terms of 'everything is now back to normal', and tended to couch the situation in much softer terms; specifically for these people.

The round table discussion that night, which was really an exercise in bashing the Authority management and having a sideswipe at perceived lack of Government action/support/financial backing on the way through, ended with a comment that astounded me.

"Why," one person asked, "don't people (media) come and talk to us, why haven't we been allowed to tell our story?"

They felt they had been ignored in the wake of Port Arthur,

and had never been able to explain their role in it. Well the answer was simple – and went back to when some of this same group of people had had their news conference in Hobart Town Hall on the Wednesday after the shootings.

I clearly recall that they did that conference only because the media had been hounding and badgering for some of those involved to tell their stories. The idea was that the conference would take place and there would be no further talking to the media until these people decided the time was right for them.

I was never informed that the time was right and until that October night I had dutifully, and in all good faith, informed any media inquiring that "they have still not indicated they want to talk".

Maybe it was crossed wires or lack of clear communication, but I, and others who informed the media that these people were still not ready to talk openly, did so with the best of intentions, to safeguard and protect them, nothing else.

It was a long drive home from the Peninsula that night.

On the way I got to thinking about one of the claims this group had made about the "police destroying the audio tapes of the radio communications on the afternoon and night of the Port Arthur massacre".

I found this to be a little over the top. The police would not deliberately destroy what would have been historic information and an important tool for the prosecution that would inevitably follow.

But they were convinced the tapes had been deliberately destroyed and that some evidence of actions they claim did or did not happen was destroyed with them. The fact is the tapes were indeed lost, but as in every good story if there is a choice between a conspiracy and a stuff up, go for the stuff up every time, and that is just what happened here.

The police do run logger tapes, similar to those in radio stations, simply to check what has happened and to have a record for themselves and for history.

But the night of April 28, 1996, was not a usual night. It was in fact hell on earth for the police radio operators and those extra people in and around the operations that night.

My understanding was that routinely, as in radio, the tape is changed at some particular time and another is put in its place. Apparently what happened that night was that the person changing the tape took off the old one, and instead of putting on a new one, simply reversed it, and put it back on the reel.

Unfortunately it was not a double sided tape, so the previous afternoon and night's tape was lost. No conspiracy just a simple accident which I have seen happen countless times in radio stations.

But those who believed the tapes had been lost or destroyed for sinister reasons will not accept this reasonable and rational explanation, and over time this has become one of the conspiracy myths surrounding Port Arthur.

Mr Bugg had done his work well and by early September I was being roped in to dealing with the media aspect of the pending court appearances and subsequent Supreme Court trial of Martin Bryant. Oh what a job, especially when at the same time you are also press secretary to the Premier.

Bryant by now of course was being held safely in the hospital wing of Risdon Prison. Special arrangements had to be made to accommodate him and special attention had to be paid to him by the prison officers, simply to keep him alive.

He was a difficult person in the early days of his incarceration, glorying in his notoriety. After recovering from his burns he tried to make friends with other inmates in the hospital, but had no idea how to go about it.

For instance, he enjoyed asking some if they knew what it was like to shoot a kid in the head at close range and wanting to compare crimes with them so he could brag that he had killed thirty-five people and so by any accounts he must be the 'baddest' guy in the prison. At another stage he decided that maybe he should be a sperm donor so as there could be more people like him in the world. The prison officers had constant battles keeping Bryant away from bragging to the wrong inmates.

Apparently in prison, it is not the done thing to skite about what crimes you have committed. No doubt there would have been a big line of inmates in Risdon who would have relished the chance to kill the worst killer in Australian history.

Several times in the first few months Bryant allegedly tried to kill himself. I say allegedly because although they were treated by staff as real attempts at suicide, it was never something that was going to happen in prison in those first few months.

Again, as at Port Arthur, Bryant couldn't manage it, mainly because he didn't really try. What he was doing again was seeking to be the centre of attention with everyone, particularly the media. And unfortunately even at this time the media could not get enough of him.

He was under 24 hour surveillance and kept in a separate wing of the hospital for about seven months, and so was unlikely to come to any real harm, but it does conjure up a conundrum doesn't it. Here you have a person accused of killing thirty-five people, and the State has to make all efforts to keep him alive and ensure that he goes to trial, so that if convicted he can spend the rest of his days in jail.

I felt, and still do feel, for the prison officers charged with looking after Bryant, who quickly became a fat slothful slob with absolutely no prospects and who, believe it or not, still had people who idolise him. In particular, there was a young woman who came to Hobart from Sydney and ingratiated herself with Bryant's mother and insisted on wanting to visit him in jail.

The mother could not get rid of this young woman, who, at one stage, actually rang the jail asking for permission to visit. Checks were made and Mrs Bryant was spoken to about this approach. She explained the situation and the visit was refused.

Apart from this sort of thing, Bryant still gets huge amounts of mail from all over the country – he answers very little, if any of it, but it keeps coming. Many writers apparently feel sorry for him and believe he has been made a scapegoat and has in some way been set up and wrongly convicted.

How naive is that? There has been no mistake in Bryant being locked up forever – and if there is to be pity or sympathy, let's think about the victims of his horror day out that Sunday.

The Chief Justice of Tasmania, Mr William John Ellis Cox was to handle the Bryant trial, and he was immediately aware of the local, national and international interest such an event was bound to generate, and very early on was involved in the necessary arrangements.

Mr Cox had been appointed Chief Justice only in September

the previous year, succeeding Sir Guy Green, who had resigned to become Governor of Tasmania. Mr Cox had been appointed a Judge of the Supreme Court of Tasmania in February, 1982.

I was asked to advise on, and put in place, the media arrangements that I thought appropriate for the occasion, and to implement the Chief Justice's wishes in this area.

Security arrangements for the trial were enormous. I attended many meetings between the Police, the Prison Service, the Court staff, the Hobart City Council (regarding parking arrangements etc) to finalise just what would be needed.

Before the first appearance of Bryant in court, a bullet proof glass petition was built around the 'dock' where he would be seated each day – and security arrangements in and around the Supreme Court building were intense, to say the least.

All contingencies had to be covered, and yet the media, again in line with Premier Rundle's instructions, were to be given every assistance in covering the trial proceedings. Remember, no one at this stage was sure what Bryant was going to do by way of plea – would it be guilty, not guilty, not guilty by reason of insanity, or not fit to enter a plea.

These were all possibilities, and the world media would again be on hand to see what unfolded and of course, each and every one of them would want a seat in the court room when Bryant was appearing.

Having worked on media arrangements for Royal Visits to Tasmania, I decided the best way to handle the Bryant court appearances was to take a similar approach to those events. To that end, I produced a media handbook for those who would be attending.

This outlined all the arrangements that had been made, and also gave them information they would need for their stories, such as biographies, on the judge, prosecutor and defence counsel.

Space was going to be a problem, and became much more so when the Chief Justice issued his decision on seat allocations in Court 7, which was to be where Bryant would appear. He decided that there would be twenty seats available each day for members of the public, to be allocated on a first come first served basis.

Mr Cox did not want the public locked out of the court while justice was being done, and I think he is to be applauded for the decision. He also allocated seats for Port Arthur survivors who might be called as witnesses (again about twenty), and this left a total of eighteen seats for the media in Court 7.

It was left to me to allocate the media seating and there was simply no way everyone was going to be happy.

In an effort to try to ensure everyone got everything from the court hearings, it was decided that the adjacent Court 8 would be set up with video link from Court 7. This would provide room for another eighty members of the media to work from Court 8 – seeing and hearing everything in Court 7 as it happened, but without actually being in that Courtroom.

It was the best that could be done under the circumstances and I think it was a sensible solution to a difficult problem. But let me say, as I had predicted, or perhaps feared, many were unhappy with the final arrangements. They couldn't see why the general public should be admitted to Court 7 and they, the media could not get a seat. I thought that was a quaint way of thinking.

I must say however, that at one stage in the early planning, someone suggested that the video link be sent from the court to a large room in a nearby hotel. To this, I proffered advice that such a move would not be acceptable because the media would want to be at the Court complex, not at some anonymous hotel.

Much the same as they went to Port Arthur to cover the original crime, rather than do it from Hobart. And it is things like this that prove the value of having an experienced media person work on such events.

It certainly helps prevent a lot of unnecessary problems, and you can picture me trying to tell those who were unhappy that they were not in Court 7 that they had to actually go away somewhere else to a hotel to watch the trial by video. It wouldn't have been pretty.

As an interesting little aside, I can tell you that for the first Bryant appearance (30th September) we had to use much smaller television screens in Court 8 than had been anticipated. What had happened was that it was a late decision to set up the video link and all the bigger television screens for hire had already been snapped up by people wanting to watch the AFL Grand Final – we got bigger screens for the later court appearances.

Given the security arrangements being put in place, I sent faxes to all the major media outlets in Australia informing them that if they were to cover the court appearances, they would need special accreditation which they could obtain through my office.

They had to nominate their staff and send passport sized pictures of them for inclusion on the laminated pass which we made up in Hobart once the police finished their scrutiny of all those nominated. Again, this is normal procedure with Royal Visits and the system worked well for the Bryant trial.

As the date of the first court appearance neared (30 Sept), I had to sit down and decide how best to allocate the media seats in Courtroom 7. It was not going to be easy – we had about 100 media people coming for the event and each of them had applied for a seat in the Court. This meant I had eighteen seats and five times that many who wanted to be there. And then I came across another problem – each of the newspapers wanted their artists to do sketches of Bryant during the appearances and so wanted extra seats.

The Chief Justice made it clear there would be no extra seats – eighteen was the media allocation. So I decided the seats on the basis that firstly, it was a local story, and therefore the local media indeed deserved priority. Secondly, it was an Australian story and national media required access and thirdly, that if any local Tasmanian newspaper had turned up at the O.J. Simpson trial, would they get inside the court? The answer was no, and so the international media would not have any special rights in Hobart.

As for the needs of the newspapers for artist drawings of Bryant, we solved that by calling the University of Tasmania Art School and seeking out a student who could handle the task. The University pointed us towards Sarah Mason, and we had her come and talk about the job we proposed.

After outlining what was needed we took her to the court room to actually see it, and get a feel for what it would be like on the day. Understandably, she was a little nervous and apprehensive about the size of the task but otherwise confident of doing a good job and could get a good likeness of Bryant on paper.

We negotiated a fee for the job and she was then appointed Court Artist for Court 7 with the arrangement being that her work would be provided by colour scan immediately after the appearance of Bryant, to all television and newspapers, which needed them.

Other artists were however, free to be in Court 8, or indeed if the newspaper or television reporter in Court 7 wanted to give up their seat to their artist, that would be allowable.

On that basis then, the seats were allocated to the *Hobart Mercury, Launceston Examiner, Burnie Advocate, WIN Television, Southern Cross Television, ABC-TV, ABC Radio,* the Hobart representative of *Australian Associated Press,* the Hobart representative of the *Sydney Morning Herald,* and the Hobart representative of the *Australian*. This covered the local media in Tasmania.

The other seats went to *Channel 7, Channel 9, Channel 10, Radio 3AW* and *2UE* and the *Herald Sun* from Melbourne. Internationally, *Reuters* wire service was allocated a seat and the court appointed artist made up eighteen.

Sarah Mason was actually very dedicated to her task. Although only told about it just days before the court appearance, she spent several hours in the court before September 30, getting background features on paper and working on colours. This stood her in good stead on the day because what happened on the 30th was that the appearance was very brief and really tested the ability of any artist who would have been expecting much more time to do the work.

As already pointed out, security in and around the court was phenomenal. The contempt of court from the magistrate's court appearance of Bryant earlier, where a photo was taken of him off a television screen, led to a real clampdown on 30 September, and for subsequent appearances. All cameras were banned from the entire Supreme Court complex simply, no cameras were allowed inside the building.

For differing reasons, but also linked to security, tape recorders, mobile phones, brief cases and hand bags were also banned from the court. The media was told that basically all they needed to bring, because it was all that would be allowed in, was pens and paper.

There was some complaint about such a crackdown and some media criticised such tight security, but it was deemed necessary by the police, and in the end they were responsible for making sure Bryant got from jail to the court and back again safely, and so it was put in place.

It didn't really cause the media any real problems apart from slight inconvenience. But I don't know if any of them had read reports about at that time, of the Israeli secret service taking out one of their targets by putting a bomb in his mobile phone. Tasmanian police were not risking anyone getting into the court and throwing a similar object at Bryant.

The Court complex was bomb searched and sealed before each appearance and people had to pass through metal detectors to get into the building. Salamanca Place was not closed to traffic while Bryant was in court but parking was limited and strictly policed.

The Chief Justice also determined that the media could have a copy of the transcript of proceedings at a fee of 50 cents per page. The transcript was a big seller, because the media wanted to get every word that was said, exactly right.

With upwards of 100 media in town, Salamanca Place outside the Supreme Court was swarming with people early on the morning of the 30th September for the long awaited and much talked about Bryant appearance. Not only media, but police and Special Operations Group officers and Bomb Squad officers were busy going through their routines to ensure all arrangements were in place.

Surprisingly, very few members of the general public turned up outside the court that day to see Bryant arrive at the complex. I must admit that I thought the very notoriety of Bryant would have attracted some people to come out and have a look at him for themselves; sort of natural curiosity. In hindsight, I think most Tasmanians had had enough of Bryant by that time.

He was brought from the prison in a special convoy with arrangements in place to ensure he got to the court early and safely.

I told the assembled media that morning that the convoy would be moving quickly and that they should not stand on the road in front of the lead vehicles to take pictures as they approached the court, because it is unlikely, for security reasons that those vehicles will stop. Some thought I was joking, but I wasn't and one mainland cameraman who must have had cloth ears found that out just a few minutes later.

As the convoy swept down Salamanca Place, the plan was for the lead vehicles to continue past the garage entrance to the Supreme Court to ensure nothing untoward could happen as the prison van turned into the parking area. The cameraman, despite warnings about what would happen, stepped out into the middle of the road in front of the lead cars – they didn't slow down and he had to scramble back to safety, yelling at the cars as they went past him.

He wanted to make an issue of the incident, until he was reminded that he had been warned and that even if he took security measures as a joke, those involved in making sure nothing happened to Bryant didn't. On future court appearances, I noticed he never stepped into the path of the cars again.

The smallish courtroom was packed for Bryant's appearance and there was a general feeling among the media that he would plead guilty. After all, hadn't the *Mercury* already published his picture on the front page and said "This is the man".

Special arrangements had been made for people from Port Arthur to enter the court and most came in a large group up the front steps of the building shortly before 10 am. They walked quickly and with dignity but the support for each other was obvious.

There was an uneasy, almost unreal feeling in the court as Bryant would, for the first time since 28th April, shortly be facing some of those who suffered dreadful losses of loved ones, or who had suffered horrible injuries from his weapons. They would be separated only by a solid glass panel and there was much emotion evident in the court as the Port Arthur people prepared to hear what Bryant would say to the charges.

The media was also a big player in the day's events – but they too were feeling the emotion in Court 7.

Damian Bugg QC and Nick Perks were appearing for the Crown and David Gunson was appearing for Bryant, but at 10 am, the appointed time for the hearing, they were not yet at their desks, but rather were apparently in conference with the Chief Justice.

There was a short delay to the start of the hearing, the reason for which was not made obvious at the time, and for which many people may still not be aware. But with the legal teams now at their desks, the media anxiously awaiting the start of proceedings, the public gallery seats full and four rows of Port Arthur survivors and their supporters looking on, Bryant was brought into the court by security guards who stood either side of him.

He was a singularly unimpressive individual, who looked much like a schoolboy who had been caught smoking behind the toilets, and was now about to be punished by the headmaster. He didn't look like a mass murderer.

There was some initial muttering amongst the Port Arthur people – some couldn't look at him immediately, others mouthed comments towards him, others tried desperately to make eye contact with him. The air was thick and the silence and stillness in the courtroom seemed surreal. In fact the whole scene conjured up images of a movie set about to do a take, only this was real.

Mr Justice Cox entered the court from behind his bench and took his seat and after the preliminary introductions by the legal teams, his associate stood and started to read.

"Prisoner at the Bar, you stand charged by the name of Martin Bryant with a first count, that of murder, contrary to Section 158 of the Criminal Code in that you, at Port Arthur on the 28th day of April, 1996, murdered David Martin, how say you, are you guilty or not guilty?"

There was a collective holding of breath by most in the court that day before the answer quickly, but very quietly came back. "Not guilty."

A brief silence, and then the Associate continued with a second count of murder, that of David Martin's wife, Noelene

Joyce Martin.

Again, "Not guilty."

The media was now writing furiously and trying to capture for their readers, viewers and listeners, the atmosphere as it existed at the time, but I don't think it was possible to actually do so. It was the sort of thing that you needed to have been there to feel.

As the "not guilty" replies continued, the radio reporters scrambled to get out and report the news – this would mean a full trial and this would mean drawn out and gruesome details of Australia's worst murder spree being aired in open court.

The 26th count "that of murder, in that at Port Arthur in Tasmania on the 28th day of April, 1996, you murdered Nicole Louise Burgess, how say you, are you guilty or not guilty?"

Not guilty again the reply.

When I first started writing this account, I believed that John and Sue Burgess had been in court that day. It was only when Sue kindly did the original proof reading of this manuscript that I realised they were not. They were at a later hearing.

To charges 50, 51 and 52, the murders of Nanette Mikac, Madeline Mikac and Alannah Mikac – Bryant again pleaded not guilty – but appeared unable to stifle a laugh as he replied to the Associate.

I don't claim to know exactly what Bryant was doing at this instant, but my reading of it was that the enormity of his whole murderous day had suddenly dawned on him and he realised what had happened. He realised what he had done.

It was a nervous rather than a confident stifled laugh that an intellectually challenged schoolboy would utter when facing the headmaster for punishment for smoking. Only this time it wasn't smoking, he wasn't a schoolboy, he was a mass murderer.

On and on it went until the count of murdering Glen Pears, to which Bryant again replied, not guilty. This was too much for Glen's brother who called from the body of the court, "You're a bloody coward, Bryant."

This shocked the public and the media, and most others in the court, but was not really something one could say was unexpected. Indeed I would not have been surprised had it happened at any one of the earlier counts.

But Mr Justice Cox never flinched. He simply looked directly down his courtroom and firmly said "you leave the room please" which the brother did, but on his way out, again called to Bryant "yours will come, son". Bryant didn't seem to react in any way to the interjections.

Mr Cox then instructed his Associate to "put the last count of the indictment to him".

"Prisoner at the bar, you stand charged with a seventy second count, that of arson contrary to section 268 of the Criminal Code in that you at Port Arthur in Tasmania on the 29th day of April, 1996, unlawfully set fire to a building to wit the dwelling Seascape, the property of David and Noelene Martin. How do you say, are you guilty or not guilty."

"Not guilty," Bryant said.

Mr Cox set the trial for 19 November, but then listed the case again for mention the following Friday with Bryant not required to appear, but to monitor preparations.

"Let him stand down," Mr Cox said, and Bryant was taken away.

Bryant was charged with nearly 70 offences in all, including

35 of murder, 20 of attempted murder, several charges of wounding and the arson of Seascape.

At this stage I must admit to wondering what the *Mercury* newspaper staff would be thinking about a not guilty plea because the picture they published before Bryant was even charged ensured that everyone in Tasmania knew who killed the thirty-five people at Port Arthur, so it raised questions about the possibility of a fair trial in Tasmania.

The convoy was reassembled and the prison van driven past the assembled media again, back to jail.

Bryant apparently decided at the last moment to plead not guilty because he wanted the notoriety of having the case go to trial and for him to gain the massive publicity it would generate. My understanding is that just before he left the prison for his first appearance, he was told by some of the old lags there that he "shouldn't plead guilty, make them prove you did it".

True or false, I don't know, but that is what he did.

The listing of the case for mention the next Friday was important because after the not guilty pleas on the Monday, David Gunson resigned as Bryant's lawyer. Bryant's plea of not guilty left Mr Gunson with no honourable alternative.

On 4th October, John Avery appeared in the Supreme Court to say "if your Honour pleases, I am now instructed to appear for the accused".

Mr Avery gave assurances that he would still be ready, despite the short notice of taking over the defence, to proceed with the trial on November 19. But things moved quickly from the time Avery took over the case, and soon there was speculation that Bryant would be changing his plea. Indeed, there was a hearing in the Supreme Court on 7th November, 1996, ostensibly to resolve a number of matters and points of law before the trial formally got under way.

After the opening formalities, Mr Cox said that he "noted Mr Avery that this is your first appearance with your client in this court".

Avery replied that "yes it would be apparent, your Honour that on the previous occasion other counsel appeared and as this is the first occasion I have appeared with my client, I think it appropriate and indeed instructive that the indictment be put to him again".

"Yes, very well, I will instruct the Clerk of the Court to put the indictment to the accused. Would you stand, Mr Bryant" Mr Cox said.

Again those in the court, under the same arrangements as the previous hearing on 30th September, listened to the first count of the murder of David Martin. How do you say, are you guilty or not guilty?

There was a slight pause before the word "guilty" came back. The relief of everyone was obvious.

The court agreed to change the pleas and Damian Bugg indicated that the trial could go ahead on 19th November and would take about two days. Bryant was again remanded in custody with Mr Justice Cox dismissing him from the court with the words "let him stand down" – and again he was taken away.

From a journalist's point of view it was interesting that before he adjourned the court that day, Mr Justice Cox issued a detailed warning to the media about what they should and should not do in the next few weeks in relation to reporting about Bryant and the upcoming trial.

It was a clear instruction that he would not tolerate any shabby journalism leading up to the trial and that anyone who transgressed would be severely dealt with. Bear in mind that at this stage, Tasmania was still afloat in Port Arthur stories. There were all sorts of television and newspapers and magazine reporters desperately digging about to get their 'scoop' interviews about the 28th April.

Mr Cox had obviously seen the *Mercury* front page picture of Bryant before he had been charged and was keen that there be no similar problems in the lead up to the trial.

Interestingly, that *Mercury* picture was the subject of investigation by Mr Bugg but for some reason it was never announced why there was no prosecution, or even if it had been indeed, a contempt of court.

In his address that day, Mr Cox said in part...

> *"That notwithstanding the accused's plea of guilty to all counts on the indictment, these proceedings are by no means over. There remains a requirement that the Crown publicly state facts upon which it relies. There remains a requirement that the accused be afforded full opportunity to place before me all facts and circumstances relevant to a plea in mitigation. Finally, it will be for me to determine, in the light of the materials placed before me the appropriate sentence.*
>
> *"The same degree of restraint in relation to the publication of material having the tendency to prejudice the outcome of court proceedings as is required prior to a trial is accordingly*

required in relation to all other matters still the subject of possible evidence, submission and resolution.

"It is important in the interests of justice that the public perception of the relevant facts upon which judgement is finally pronounced should be formed on proper reporting of that material when it is presented to the court and should not be distorted by premature publication of untested and possibly incorrect accounts or opinions.

"Anyone who deliberately engages in any activity which brings this remaining process into jeopardy or which prejudices in any way the just conclusion of these proceedings in accordance with the law will commit a grave contempt of this court and can expect prosecution and condign punishment if proven to be guilty of it" he said.

It all seemed to make the situation pretty clear, even for the most gung ho of journalists who might have been tempted to run their own Trial of Bryant ahead of that to be conducted by Mr Cox.

The trial proper began on 19 November, 1996, and again it was the biggest show in town. Hobart was swamped by media from around the nation, and this time most of the international agencies took their feeds on the trial from Australian media.

However, the French Newsagency, *AFP,* did in the weeks leading up to the trial try valiantly to get a seat in Court 7. There were letters from Australian editors and other executives explaining that *AFP* was a major international agency and therefore deserved a seat in the court for the trial.

Unfortunately for the journalist they had decided to send to

Hobart, the waters for her had been fairly well muddied by the cameraman they sent to cover the Magistrate's Court appearance of Bryant and where he took a photo from the video screen. *AFP* was not allocated a seat in Court 7.

As with the earlier appearances, security in and around the court was massive for the trial, and again the convoy made its way each day from Risdon Prison to the court complex.

And being just as predictable the media again had to film and photograph every entry and exit the prison van made, even though the windows had been blacked out, mostly for security reasons. It always amuses me that although there is no chance whatsoever of getting a usable shot, cameramen and photographers feel duty bound to take pictures of blacked out windows anyway.

Damian Bugg QC for the Crown opened the case by simply stating the facts. They were brutally succinct.

"Your Honour, Martin Bryant has pleaded guilty to all counts in the indictment which was filed in this court on 5th July.

"On the 28th April this year he travelled to Port Arthur. He drove there in his Volvo sedan which at the time had a surfboard placed on the roof racks of the car. The Crown's case is that at the outset of that journey he intended at least some form of violent confrontation with Mr and Mrs Martin of the Seascape tourist accommodation facility at Port Arthur and in all probability his intentions also extended to actions which had the devastating impact on the community and people of Port Arthur that day.

"I say this because on the Crown case he had made

preparations which were inconsistent with his normal behaviour. He behaved deceptively to those close to him as to his possession and use of firearms. They were concealed in his house in the body of two pianos and elsewhere within the house out of view of visitors to that property. His acts of preparation included buying a sports bag to conceal one of his weapons, he took handcuffs with him, rope and a hunting knife and three semi automatic weapons and a significant quantity of ammunition.

"He followed through a series of actions which culminated in a hostage and siege situation which had an air of pre-planning. He clearly intended to embark upon violence and murderous conduct of the type to which he has pleaded guilty."

"Bryant at the time lived comfortably in the sense that he didn't have any money worries. His lifestyle was different and his behaviour, in the eyes of many, inappropriate. He owned and drove a motor vehicle but did not possess a driver's licence. He owned and on the 28th April used military style semi-automatic weapons but did not hold a licence or any form of authorisation to possess or own these weapons. A search of his house at Clare Street after the shootings at Port Arthur revealed that he had hidden the firearms in the house and had other weapons and ammunition concealed there in such a way that his girlfriend and other visitors would not be able to locate them. He was obviously stockpiling those weapons and ammunition which had a disturbing killing efficiency".

Bryant sat quietly in the court as Mr Bugg continued outlining the facts against him. Often he asked for a glass of water as he, maybe for the first time, had his full actions of that day explained to him.

He also at times looked around the court to see who was there and no doubt recognised many of the Port Arthur people who were affected by this atrocity. At no time though during the trial did I detect any hint or evidence that he was remorseful or sorry about what he had done.

Mr Bugg signalled his intentions in regard to sentencing submissions early on the first day of the trial.

"I will because of the substantial number of murders committed by this man be submitting that in relation to the counts of murder to which he has pleaded guilty the sentence of life imprisonment is the only appropriate sentence on those convictions and that your Honour's discretion under the Parole Act should be exercised by orders under section 12B(a) that he is not eligible for parole in respect of that sentence".

And then he launched into the Crown case against Bryant which had been meticulously put together in the previous couple of months. It was a difficult task to get such a mountain of evidence together for presentation to the court in such a short time. However, it was in the interests of everyone to have the case resolved before the end of 1996. I am sure all those closely associated with the case will agree that a speedy resolution was the best outcome.

"*Bryant's home in Clare Street is fitted with an electronic alarm system. In attending, the police late in the day of the 28th April discovered that the alarm had been set, that is, engaged at 9.47 that morning. So obviously that was the time at which Bryant left his home.*

"*He was driving his yellow Volvo sedan and carrying with him at the time the AR-15 semi-automatic point 223 calibre rifle and an FN, commonly called an SLR military style semi automatic point 308 calibre rifle and a semi automatic Daiwoo 12 gauge shotgun. He also had with him two sets of handcuffs, sashcord rope and a hunting knife and a number of containers of petrol*".

Those in the court sat transfixed as Bugg and his assistant Nick Perks revealed the case against Bryant and were amazed at the minute detail the Crown was able to expose.

Mr Bugg spent much of the first morning's session detailing the various counts against Bryant and outlining just how he had massacred the people in the Broad Arrow restaurant.

He described a chilling scene with a gunman deliberately shooting people, mostly in the head, while at the time "laughing in an aggressive way rather than an amused way".

Not even seasoned court reporters were ready for the details of Mr Bugg's submission. They were excruciating in their detail and described the full horror and fear felt by people trapped in the cafe and elsewhere that April afternoon.

Shortly after the morning break Mr Bugg moved to have the remains of the rifle used in the killings, the AR-15 semi automatic

.223 removed from the court and returned to the police safe, away from the sight of those in the court that day who survived the massacre.

"The weapon is very light, it is a semi automatic, not fully automatic and has a 30 shot magazine and there is apparent damage to it because it was recovered by police from the Seascape ruins the next day" he said.

Mr Justice Cox had the weapon and magazine identified MFI-A for the court records, and then it was removed from the courtroom.

Mr Bugg then moved to have two videos played to the court, to highlight the time frame in which so many people died in the Broad Arrow Cafe – this I think was what really pushed home the message of the horror of Port Arthur that day.

The first showed Bryant entering his car and about to leave the car park area, the second was much more dramatic.

It had been taken from the Penitentiary area of the Historic Site and it was significant because of the noise level which can be heard of the gun fire from the cafe, some 200 metres away. The two tapes were in fact the recording of the gunshots fired from the moment Bryant took the gun out of the sports bag and started shooting in the cafe.

Mr Bugg explained, *"The first tape stopped after 15 seconds and it recorded seventeen shots. The second tape was, as far as the sounds of the shots in the cafe is concerned, stopped after 23 seconds and recorded twenty-one shots.*

"But if one goes back to the first tape, which stopped recording after 15 seconds, in those 15 seconds twelve people

were dead, one had suffered grievous bodily harm, five were wounded and four had suffered significant injuries in Bryant's attempts to murder them.

"I will come back to the numbers of shots fired and what occurred at the end of an examination of the criminal behaviour of this man in the cafe that afternoon.

"Bryant continued towards the souvenir shop area of the building. Working in this area of the shop that day were Nicole Burgess and Elizabeth Howard. Bryant moved towards the souvenir area, he shot Nicole Burgess; she was standing near the counter. He was standing some distance from her when he shot her and the shot struck her in the head, she fell forwards, the injuries caused were immediately fatal".

Through their tears, John and Sue Burgess supported each other at this public recounting of the horrific detail of the death of their child.

Throughout the day the evidence continued, as the Crown case built.

Mr Bugg went on *"Your Honour, it is hard to express in any finite terms the precise period of time Bryant was in the cafe but I would put to this court that he was in there for approximately one and a half to, at the outside, two minutes, whilst he was firing his gun.*

"In that time he killed twenty people, attempted to kill four, wounded six and caused grievous bodily harm to one. He fired twenty-nine shots. Very few of them missed a target,

and most of them struck targets when fired at either point blank or close range. There is absolutely no doubt as to his intent and his desire to cause maximum carnage.

"Mr Perks and I were discussing the appropriate term for his conduct, and wondered about the appropriateness of execution and concluded that it was more appropriate to term what he did in that cafe as slaughter."

The Crown then dealt with Bryant's movements outside the cafe where he continued to murder people; and I got the feeling that the media were being a bit overwhelmed by the magnitude of the crime and the detail of the evidence being presented.

It was certainly hard for those people who had lost loved ones on that Sunday to sit through the trial evidence that morning, and probably none more so than Walter Mikac. Walter of course had his wife and two daughters murdered by Bryant and his dignified manner in coping with such a tragedy has been an inspiration to many around Australia.

Mr Bugg eventually had to deal with Bryant's murder of Mrs Mikac and her daughters on the road near the Toll Booth as he made his way out of the Port Arthur Historic Site.

The evidence was not easy to listen to, and just as hard to read.

"There were other people in this area at the same time, all trying to make their way out of the site. Mrs Boskovic spoke to Alanna, to calm her down, Mrs Mikac then said to her daughter, 'We're safe now, Pumpkin,' and the child appeared to relax and moved closer to her mother. At this time the yellow Volvo was being driven up Jetty road towards the Toll

Booth. Bryant stopped the vehicle opposite Mrs Mikac and she then started to approach the vehicle. It was fairly obvious that Mrs Mikac must have thought that this vehicle would provide some escape from the area.

"At this moment Bryant alighted from the car. Witnesses observed Bryant to place his left hand on Mrs Mikac's shoulder and people were close enough to hear him tell her to get down on her knees on three occasions. Mrs Mikac was then heard to say, 'Please don't hurt my babies.'

"Another couple in the area noticed Alannah, the elder of the two children run to hide behind a tree off the roadside. One of these people saw Bryant point the rifle at Mrs Mikac and fire once. She fell to the ground.

"The Crown case is that Bryant shot Mrs Mikac in the left side of the head. Death was immediate. Almost immediately after this he has fired at Madeline, he fired two shots at the child. The first shot struck the child in the right shoulder and the second shot to the chest and abdomen caused fatal massive internal injuries.

"Bryant then turned his attention on Alannah. It appears that he fired two shots at the child, she was sheltering behind a tree off to the side of the road at a distance of about 5.5 metres and those first two shots were fired from somewhere near his car. He then moved to the tree and shot her at near contact point with the muzzle almost pressed against the right side of the child's neck.

"Bryant then re-entered his vehicle and drove on towards the toll booth."

Remember, this is the same person who at his first court appearance where he pleaded not guilty to the thirty-five murders 'giggled' when the Mikac cases were put to him.

At the lunch break there appeared to be none of the usual rush by the media to get out and file their stories, they had absorbed the evidence and as I said, some were being a bit overwhelmed in hearing the facts for the first time.

Usually in high profile court cases, there is a scramble by media crews at any break to get new pictures and photos of those involved – this time however, there was a seeming reluctance to become too intrusive.

We had made arrangements for the media to get the information they required and we had asked them not to harass those most closely involved, and for the most part, on day one of the trial, they did not go overboard.

That isn't to say some didn't ask silly questions of survivors, such as "how do you feel about the evidence being given", but this time they were happy not to get an answer. It seems they felt compelled for some reason to ask the question, but didn't repeat it if there was no reply.

Nick Perks, who was assisting Damian Bugg preparing the Crown case, also deserves enormous credit for his efforts.

He was the one who handled all the photographic evidence that helped to build the case. You only need to cast your mind back to the evidence about what happened in the Broad Arrow Cafe to understand some of the pictures he was forced to study, day in and day out, in putting the prosecution case together. It was not easy and the stress and strain of it all did show two nights later after Bryant had been sentenced.

During the afternoon session of the court on the first day, the Crown presented evidence of Bryant's murderous departure from Port Arthur and his return trip to Seascape holiday accommodation.

On the way out of the site he killed another dozen people, taking the toll for that Sunday to thirty-two. He also took with him a hostage who was later to be killed; and he had already killed the Martins.

Before the start of the hearing that morning, I had noticed a dark haired young lady approach the Court Complex. She had her arm in a sling and I learned later that she was Linda White from Victoria. In dealing with the survivors of Port Arthur at the hearing, I got to know her over the next couple of days and she also had a story to tell. But hers was one which will make most of the media cringe and from which she could get no redress at the time. Hopefully, albeit some time after the event, I can help expose what was done to her in the name obviously, of ratings.

But firstly you need to know Linda's story.

As told to the Supreme Court on 19th November, 1996, "Linda White was driving an aqua Holden Frontera four wheel drive vehicle towards Port Arthur on Sunday, 28th April, and was passing Seascape just as Bryant arrived back there from the Historic Site.

"Sitting beside her was her boyfriend, now fiancé, Michael Wanders. As their vehicle approached the Seascape driveway, Miss White, whose attention had initially been directed at the beauty of the Seascape cottages and their tranquil setting noticed the BMW (Bryant had stolen it

from Port Arthur), on the left hand side of the road and standing by it a young blonde haired male. As she drove closer she noticed he had a long gun by his sides. She thought at the time that he must have been waiting for them to pass so that he could shoot rabbits or something. She slowed down further. When only a matter of a few metres separated them Bryant raised the firearm, pointed it directly at Miss White and fired it, attempting to kill her.

"This initial shot struck the bonnet of the vehicle just below the windscreen on the driver's side, part of the projectile fragmenting and smashing into the edge of the windscreen at head level and causing glass to strike Miss White's face.

"As the car drew level with Bryant he fired a second shot followed by a third and possibly a fourth in quick succession, shattering the front passenger and driver's side windows. One of the projectiles slammed into Miss White's right forearm, virtually blowing it away and causing horrific injury.

"The Crown case is that when Bryant discharged the second and subsequent shots he intended to kill Miss White's front seat passenger, Michael Wanders. Remarkably Mr Wanders was not physically injured.

"After passing Bryant's position, the vehicle continued down the hill and just around the bend from the Seascape entrance before rolling to a stop. Miss White at the time believed that this was because she simply couldn't drive any more due to her grievously injured arm. She and Mr Wanders both got out and swapped seats by running around the front of the car. Once in the driver's seat Mr Wanders made several desperate but unsuccessful attempts to restart

it. A later examination of the Frontera revealed the fact that the shot that had penetrated the bonnet had also severed the throttle cable.

"At about the time Mr Wanders was trying to restart the car Mr Doug Horne was approaching Seascape in a maroon Ford Falcon sedan. Also present in the vehicle was Mr Neville Shilkin in the front passenger seat. His wife, Helen was behind him in the rear seat with Mrs Faye Horne beside her.

"After first noticing the pink buildings of Seascape, Mr Horne observed the BMW parked in or near the driveway as did others in the Falcon. As their car drew nearer Mr Horne saw Bryant standing at what he thought was the front of the vehicle. Mr Shilkin yelled out, 'He's got a gun!' and at the same instant, and when the Falcon was but a few metres from him, Bryant raised the firearm to his shoulder and fired directly at Mr Horne.

"The bullet penetrated the windscreen and fragmented, shrapnel peppering Mr Horne, causing multiple wounds to the right side of his chest and right shoulder, arm, elbow and forearm. Fortuitously, neither Mrs Horne nor the Shilkins sustained injury.

"Mr Horne drove a short distance, stopping behind the Holden Frontera and then in a state of shock got out of the vehicle briefly.

"Miss White, having noticed Mr Horne's Falcon, ran towards it and tried to get in via the front passenger door. Meanwhile, Mr Horne, almost certainly not comprehending the situation or appreciating the desperate plight of Miss

White, got back behind the wheel of the Falcon and drove forward a short distance around the Frontera and stopped again just ahead of it after being told by his wife that he just couldn't drive off.

"Both Mr Horne and Mr Shilkin then got out of the vehicle and swapped positions. Miss White and Mr Wanders ran to the Falcon, Miss White getting into the rear seat and Mr Wanders the front on Mr Horne's knee.

"Mr Shilkin then drove the group to the Fox and Hounds and ultimate safety" was how Mr Bugg explained their escape to the court.

But that was just the start for Linda – her arm was shattered by the bullet from Bryant's rifle and it took some time to get her to hospital.

She told me later that when she got there the news didn't get any better.

Everyone who looked at her arm decided the best they could do was take it off; and after a time which she concedes was probably not long, just seemed like that, she began to resign herself to losing her right arm below the elbow. Not an ideal option, but seemingly the only one.

However, it turned out that one of the State's leading plastic surgeons, who had been called into the hospital to help on that Sunday night took a longer look at the damage.

While conceding the wound was horrendous, he was however, prepared to have a go at rejoining and repairing what he could so as the arm might be saved. And so Linda was off on her first in a long round of surgical operations over the coming months. The recovery has not been easy and while Linda and Mick Wanders were to get married, one section of the media I believe made merciless use of the pair.

Channel Nine was doing a 'definitive' Port Arthur documentary to be screened as soon after Bryant was sentenced as possible, and had targeted a number of people involved in the tragedy to take part.

Linda, because of her stunning good looks, her love story with Mick, her serious injury and bright and infectiously positive outlook on life was a logical person to have on such a program.

However, let's not forget that behind the facade of the public face, there is always a private person. Linda was not at all keen to tell her story but was pursued at length by the station.

She could easily have sold her story if that was the sort of person she was, but as far as I know she didn't and she agreed to do the *Channel Nine* program in the belief that it would be the only time she would need to do it, and that the program would be credible.

As Linda tells it, the interviews were done and the story cut and ready to go just as soon as Bryant was sentenced and that was turning out to be towards the end of November, remarkably just seven months after his rampage. She was happy that she would only have to go through the trauma of it all and relive the events once.

But just before she arrived in Hobart for the trial, a strange thing happened. She got a phone call from a producer at *Channel Nine* who told her it would be OK for her to do an interview with a certain reporter from a Sunday newspaper.

Linda said that "no, it wasn't OK", she had spoken to *Nine* on the basis that that was the end of it, she wasn't interested in doing any more media.

Thinking that was the end of the issue, she and Mick came to Hobart for the trial and were immediately contacted by the reporter who wanted to do a face to face interview with them, but particularly they wanted to talk to Linda.

Politely, on the first approach she declined. Not to be put off, the reporter tried again the next day, and the invitation was again declined. No amount of refusal was good enough to make the reporter understand that neither of them wanted to do an interview with him or anyone else, and finally at the end of the week he went away.

Imagine then the shock for Linda on the Sunday morning of the day the *Nine* program was to go to air to find a "face to face" interview between herself and the reporter on her experiences at and since Port Arthur.

This person never did an interview with Linda yet could publish words to indicate that he did. The answer of course had to be that someone had to have given him access to the video of the *Nine* program going to air on the Sunday night. It seems he simply took the words of Linda and inserted himself into the story as asking the questions. Not very ethical, I would have thought.

Linda was devastated – she called me at my office and was virtually in tears. Imagine how I felt when she recounted what had happened, and then said words I will never forget. She said that having this happen made her feel worse than the actual incident of being shot. It was that serious to her.

There was no redress through the television program; the

producer who had called and told her it would be OK to do the interview with the reporter refused to return her calls. How gutless was that? He must have known what he had done. But it is also another example of the lack of accountability of the media. Linda had been through absolute hell, she didn't need the media playing silly games with her life.

Out of the whole Port Arthur incident the one thing I treasure most is a Christmas card that I got that year.

It arrived at my office in the Executive Building in Hobart and the writing on the envelope had the appearance of being written by a child, and I thought it was from one of the schools I had visited with the Premier earlier in the year.

But no, it was from Linda White, and while the writing looked like that of a child, one had to remember that Linda who was right handed, was now, just seven months after being shot, learning to write with her left, and she was making a good fist of it.

It was the sort of thing, when one thinks about it, and the background to the circumstances, that brings tears to your eyes. I only wish the media people who had so cruelly betrayed her could have seen the same thing.

The card reads – "Thank you so much for the copy of the court transcripts you sent me re April 28, 1996. It was a pleasure to meet you; I only wish happier circumstances bring us together again one day. Look us up if you are ever in Melbourne. Linda White and Mick Wanders". I still carry that card in my briefcase as a reminder of how one can overcome adversity.

But back to the trial of Martin Bryant; day one ended with the evidence about Linda and Mick and the media by then were overloaded with facts and emotions.

The news bulletins that night and the papers the next day concentrated on the facts surrounding the short time Bryant took to kill so many people, and in particular, on how he killed Nanette Mikac and her daughters.

The evidence presented that day was dreadful and horrifying to the point of being numbing to those sitting in the courts and hearing it recounted, but it also needed to be made public so as the nation could understand what happened. It was also taken by the anti-gun lobby as confirmation that their stand against military style weapons had been correct.

Day two of the Supreme Court proceedings was to deal more with Bryant himself and an attempt by his lawyer John Avery to enter a plea in mitigation.

I must say that after what had been heard on the first day, any attempt by any person to put mitigating circumstances was a brave effort.

There was one interesting sidelight to the first day of the trial. When Damian Bugg introduced the video evidence, I was bombarded with requests from television stations for copies, they obviously wanted it for their news bulletins that night.

When I approached Mr Bugg about getting copies, his response was that it wasn't his to provide. It belonged to the owners who had copyright of the tapes and that the media should be approaching the owners for permission to use them.

This caused no end of frustration from all networks, except *Nine*. Yes, the same one that betrayed Linda White. It turned out they had been preparing for the Bryant trial for months and had really done their homework.

In fact they had done so much they apparently managed to do a deal with Tasmania police who gave them access to certain evidence and information which could only be used after the Trial, and this included the names of people who took the video at Port Arthur on 28th April.

Word soon got around the court that *Nine* had done "some sort of deal" but no one would confirm that for me at the time.

In fact I was hung out to dry somewhat because I kept being told that "no one had access to the tapes". Technically that was right, not until the trial was over.

So I was left to tell the media they could only get access through the rightful owners and they were not easily contactable with the short time left before the nightly news bulletins. I don't think Tasmania police did me any favours by doing what they did, and in the end, I don't think that *Nine* delivered them the gee whiz training tape they had promised in return for favoured access to information. So Linda White wasn't the only one betrayed by *Nine*.

But then again, *Nine* had done well in the ratings with their better preparation for the Bryant trial than any of the other networks and probably didn't worry too much about what they left behind in Tasmania.

The second day of Bryant's trial followed the lines of the first. Again the strict and early convoy from the prison to the holding cells under the court complex, but only after the entire precinct had again been searched by the bomb squad and other precautions taken.

The morning session brought more information about the *ABC* call to Bryant on the day of the massacre and siege.

"At about 2.10 pm that day (April 28th), Alison Smith, an ABC reporter left Hobart headed towards Port Arthur with a camera crew after hearing about the shooting incident. While travelling south, Miss Smith made a series of telephone calls on her mobile phone to various businesses in the Port Arthur area to try and glean some further information.

"Between 2.30 and 2.40 pm, she telephoned the Seascape number and Miss Smith gives this account of what happened. A male person answered the telephone and said Hullo, hullo. The male person was laughing hysterically and I again said Hullo, and he then said Hullo.

"I asked this person if I had the right number for Seascape and he laughed again and said, yes. I said who am I talking to, he laughed again and said, well, you can call me Jamie. I then said it's the ABC calling, what's happening? What's happening is I'm having lots of fun. There was a pause and he said, but I really need a shower, another pause, if you try to call me again, I'll shoot the hostage. Miss Smith could hear breathing into the telephone for a few seconds and then it cut out".

As I said earlier, Miss Smith claims she stumbled across Seascape; but by the time she was calling, I believe it was fairly common knowledge to those who have the ability to monitor police radio networks (like the media in Tasmania did at this time), that the gunman from Port Arthur had gone to ground at the Seascape holiday complex.

I knew that Seascape was being talked about as the place the gunman had gone and so on the basis of what I said above, I believe the call was made in the full knowledge that the cottages were the centre of the drama.

Indeed, if the reporter was simply trawling the phone book for Port Arthur businesses, which would probably have been closer to the Port Arthur historic site, 'S' in the directory is a lot of entries past 'P', and why would you look at 'S' anyway, unless you had some inside knowledge?

Bryant was first interviewed by police on July 4th at Risdon Prison.

During this interview which was electronically recorded, Bryant admitted ownership of the Colt AR15 rifle. He further admitted to kidnapping a male person and ordering him at gunpoint into the boot of the BMW and then driving the vehicle to Seascape and subsequently setting it on fire.

However, at all times during the interview Bryant maintained the denial that he had ever entered the Port Arthur Historic Site on 28th April, or that he had shot any person.

The court was then played an edited version of that interview as Mr Perks said "not because the Crown relies on any part of it, but because we consider that it is important that your Honour gains a proper appreciation of the accused's ability to field questions from two experienced police officers and secondly because his responses and demeanour are demonstrative of his complete lack of remorse".

I don't think the media realised at the time, but there were potentially very serious problems with the Crown case in relation to the recording of this interview. The court was told the quality of the sound and vision on the tape are not particularly good, there was some breakdown with the recording facility and the tape has been reconstructed using the sound from an audio tape which was recorded at the same time as the original interview so there was some lack of synchronisation at times and the vision is not particularly good.

Mr Justice Cox asked Bryant's lawyer, John Avery, if he had any submissions in view of the editing and substitution of some of the audio tape, to which he replied simply "I was not aware of it but I am not troubled by what's proposed your Honour".

The full Bryant interview ran for about two hours. The court was not played it all but there were some interesting facts to emerge.

Early on Bryant admits buying several weapons and paying three thousand dollars for a Daiwoo 12 gauge shotgun which he said he never got around to using because it scared him.

He told police about buying the Colt AR15 about five months before the Port Arthur shootings and of having paid five thousand dollars for it, complete with a telescopic sight, and strap and some ammunition thrown in.

Significantly, Bryant told police that "I s'pose it helps you, when you got the money it helps. People pass things over if you've got the cash".

He asked about the Hobart dealer from whom he had bought some of his guns and admitted to police he never at any stage had a gun licence. But that wasn't unusual because he also later admitted that he never had a driver's licence either.

Bryant had the money and the will to buy the firearms he used at Port Arthur and there were little or no checks at the time on who was buying what. Indeed I remember in the late 1980's being able to buy rifles at the big chain stores.

Remember this interview was early July and Bryant's comprehension of the extent of his troubles seemed somewhat limited. At one stage he was talking about how he liked to travel overseas as often as he could.

He told Inspector Ross Paine that "unfortunately I couldn't go on any more (trips) otherwise I would have gone away in May. I was informed nicely that I wasn't able to go away for a long time, for about 12 months, which upset me greatly".

Bryant's money meant he could travel overseas regularly, and he did. He enjoyed air travel especially because for those 10 or 12 hours of the trip he had, in the passengers seated beside him, a captive audience. They couldn't get away and had to listen to him.

For those who think such things are significant, it turned out that Bryant was left handed.

Bryant also seemed capable of taunting the police officers interviewing him. When telling his version of kidnapping a man and putting him into the boot of the BMW to be driven to Seascape, he commented matter of factly that "you see, if people don't do these unfortunate things, you guys wouldn't have a job to do".

But not long after this exchange, while fidgeting with the chains around his legs which were apparently aggravating his burns, he tells Inspectors Paine and Warren that "this is why I might've been better off if I wasn't alive anymore with all this, this bullshit. I wouldn't have to worry about all this would I, I wouldn't be in prison would I, but and all the burns, having to put up with the burns and stuff, be easier for you wouldn't it, if I was" (dead).

Throughout the interview Bryant continued to maintain that he wasn't at Port Arthur on 28th April, although he had an interesting answer when asked if he thought that people should accept the consequences of what they do.

"Yeah I do. I s'pose I should (do time) for a little while for what I've done. Just a while and let me out, let me live my own life. I'm missing my mum. I really miss her actually, what she cooks up for me, her rabbit stews and everything. She's not even allowed to bring a little bit of food in for me, that, that's a bit upsetting."

The Inspectors then explained to Bryant that he had been charged with thirty-five counts of murder, approximately twenty counts of attempted murder and several wounding charges as well as the arson of Seascape.

"How (many) months will it get me in?" Bryant asked.

It was only at the very end of the interview when the police officers were preparing to leave the prison, and Bryant apparently thought the electronic recording had stopped, that he came anywhere near close to making any sort of admission about the killings at Port Arthur.

He said to Inspector Paine, "I'm sure you'll find the person who caused all this. Me."

Inspector Paine replied, "I don't find that a very funny statement at all Martin, to be quite honest."

Bryant said, "You should've put that on recording."

"Oh it's still recording at this present stage, so that is on recording," Inspector Paine replied.

The Police interview with Bryant took up the morning session of the Trial's second day, and after the lunch break Damian Bugg returned to present victim impact statements.

These were new to the justice system in Tasmania and Mr Bugg gave careful thought to the words he used; and as transfixed as the media were to the morning interview with Bryant, the other side of the story unfolded in the first part of the afternoon session.

Mr Bugg clinically crystallised the impact that Bryant's rampage had had on the entire community; those in the courtroom could not escape the brutality of his actions.

> *"Your Honour, the grief and anguish that is experienced following the sudden and unexpected loss of a life's companion or a lover, a parent, a child or a cherished friend is a human emotion which requires no explanation; and in times of strife or human conflict or even natural disaster, we tend to accept loss of life or significant personal injury as one of the exigencies of the environment or times within which we live.*
>
> *"There is no everyday experience which can condition the human psyche for a violent assault upon it of the proportions of Martin Bryant's senseless criminal behaviour on 28th April, 1996. In a situation such as this I would go so far as to submit that a detailed analysis in a subjective sense of the impact of this man's callous conduct upon his victims is unlikely to increase the ultimate sentence which I submit your Honour should be moved to impose upon him.*
>
> *"But it is important that a general overview of the impact of this man's crimes upon his victims be given, not*

only to properly record in a general sense the impact of the crimes, but also to provide the victims with an opportunity to have the impact of that crime and their reactions to it made known to this court.

"Understandably there is such a mixture of human emotion in the responses provided as a response to an invitation I issued a week and a half ago, that it is impossible to individually deal with the responses of each victim. There have been expressions of anger, sorrow, emotional and physical pain, a desire for retribution, an inescapable element of the sentencing process as far as this matter is concerned, despair in coping with the void caused by these crimes and a sense of hopelessness.

"Some people have dealt with their burdens with a fierce determination to survive and a will to prove ultimately that they have been the victor, others have, in the diverse complexity of human nature, been utterly devastated by the event and with help are bravely struggling to the surface, in the middle, we see people with steady dispositions and wonderfully strong family or support groups to lean upon when the need arises.

"To outsiders these people have survived and are coping. With some few exceptions, Mr Perks, Mr Craig Coad and I have probably spoken to most people directly affected by this horrible massacre. But as I said, your Honour, it would not be appropriate to go though individually in detail the impact of the crime on each individual because I have already identified perhaps two reasons why, and one is that it would be unfair to differentiate in my submission based

on responses, and seek to provide the court some substantial differences and the reasons for them in the responses to these criminal acts.

"Your Honour, I have listed those people who suffered significant physical injury as a result of direct gunshot or relayed gunshot on 28th April. Those people have, in many instances, had to undergo a considerable number of surgical processes. They will never fully recover from the significant injuries which they have suffered as a result of this man's callous criminal conduct. Persons who suffered serious injury on that day were not only subjected to physical pain of the injury but also the anxiety and apprehension caused by the isolation of the site at which this incident occurred.

"Many waited in fear of death whilst appropriate arrangements were made to evacuate them from the area. These people experienced extreme levels of pain, anxiety and frustration and the responses of their companions can be equally understood.

"When they were eventually evacuated they were separated from their companions and this only added to the anxiety of the latter. These people have also had to undergo as I said, surgical procedures on many occasions and even now many of them are confronted with further operations and therapy.

"Some of the persons who are the subject of the attempted murder charges have suffered significant physical impairment, loss of employment, or employment prospects and certainly enjoyment of life. The impact of the crime upon injured persons also includes the need for ongoing

counselling, experience extreme grief, sleeplessness, flashbacks, nightmares, anxiety attacks which can involve nausea, loss of balance, headaches and so on. Many have become socially withdrawn and suffer anxiety when in public places, particularly restaurants.

"The emotional impact on injured persons also includes feelings of loss of identity and suffering depression sometimes to the point of having suicidal tendencies. For many their depression is exacerbated by both the pain and the limited mobility resulting from the physical injuries.

"And I should add that some of the people, and I know particularly having spoken to Miss Linda White, that the surgical procedures which have had to be undertaken to try and reconstruct the injury sites, and in her case, her arm, has itself had a huge telling effect on the sound remainder of their bodies.

"The social consequences for victims who were injured at Port Arthur include feeling isolated and losing their sense of freedom in society, loss of self esteem, social insecurity, in some cases inability to drive motor vehicles and requiring assistance in performing what previously were for them everyday tasks. Some have suffered severe financial loss due to inability to work and for many this incident has caused a significant reduction in their quality of life.

"Dealing with those who lost family members or friends the nature of the impact of the crime on the families and friends of victims include emotional, social, physical and financial harm. The emotional impact ranges from sadness and disbelief to anger and bitterness to extreme grief, in some

cases requiring hospitalisation and further to depression which for some people extended to considering suicide. Some have been prescribed anti depressant medication and sleeping tablets.

"The families of victims have expressed feelings of powerlessness and frustration, feelings of loss even for those surviving members whose lives have fallen apart. They have described their lives as being totally destroyed, feeling pain at seeing family members grieving and struggling to be strong and supportive to their loved ones.

"Many have suffered relationship breakdowns, many families and friends of the victims have expressed that they have lost their direction in life and that they are reassessing their whole lives.

"Many complained of loneliness and of feeling trapped, many who were also at Port Arthur with their now deceased loved ones suffer from recurrent nightmares and flashbacks.

"This tragedy had also impacted upon people's social existence, some victims have said they feel isolated, that they have a feeling of not being loved, of being socially insecure, some to a point of describing themselves as agoraphobic.

"Some have difficulty dealing with everyday tasks and find that they are easily prompted into a bout of uncontrollable crying and some have said they experience feelings of guilt when enjoying life. Some members of families or friends of deceased now suffer from stress, feel emotionally exhausted and some of those still working have difficulty with concentration. Some have increased or started smoking and increased their alcohol consumption.

"Many families and friends of deceased victims are receiving ongoing counselling as well. Many of the deceased victims' relatives needed to take time off work and for some that meant loss of their own income on top of loss of income from their deceased partners. Many have suffered financially as a result of the loss of income of a partner or a parent and in some cases a sibling or a son or a daughter. There are other obvious financial consequences for families of deceased victims, usually the cost of flying interstate to be with other family members or to attend funerals and so on.

"Your Honour, it goes without saying that obviously the conduct that we have described to you, particularly yesterday, would when observed by a person or when committed in the presence, perhaps without full awareness of many people, have had a significant impact upon those people. Just the realisation of how close they came themselves to suffering such violence in itself has had a shattering effect on many people. Many eye witnesses to the events of April 28th have since felt anger and bitterness, disbelief and powerlessness, some have even felt guilt at not being able to do more than they did on the day. And of course, I hope that the playing of the video tape yesterday would allay some of those concerns.

"Many eye witnesses now suffer from fear and anxiety attacks and feel socially insecure, many are particularly nervous, some even claustrophobic in crowds or public places such as shopping malls. Many eye witnesses have suffered marital breakdowns or significant tensions within their family relationships and some have expressed suicidal tendencies as well.

"A common complaint is that they keep reliving the event and that is what haunts them. Many suffer from flashbacks and have trouble sleeping. Some witnesses have suffered from weight loss or even weight gain, some have developed eating disorders.

"Many complain of tiredness and some have experienced a reduction in their general physical health and some, as I've said in relation to another group, have taken up smoking.

"It is not uncommon for witnesses to say they lose their temper more readily than they used to. For some violence has become a problem for them within their own homes and for others any sign of violence or even loud noise becomes extremely distressing. An illustration of that has been given by some witnesses as to their reaction to the sounds of helicopters. Many witnesses have become more security conscious and are aware of noises. Some have been concerned at driving and feeling isolated and many have said that as a result of this incident they have lost their trust in many people. Many expressed distress over their feeling of total lack of control at the time of the event.

"The impact upon children has also been significant. Changes in results and performances at school have been observed for the worse.

"Insofar as the general community is concerned, your Honour, I propose to merely rely upon your Honour's own perception, having lived within this community during the last six months, as to the impact it has had in a global sense within this State, but obviously, and it goes without saying, that the emergency services personnel, ambulance, *police officers, employees at Port Arthur historic site, hospital employees and people directly connected with dealing with this tragedy have all be subjected to a most unusual, even for their training, experience within their work and responsibility.*

"For those people, some have suffered sleeplessness and other understandable responses to the stress of having to maintain control and deal with this tragic event.

"Your Honour, just before moving on, there was one passage from a written response which I proposed to just conclude this aspect of the Crown's presentation to you and it is a response from one person who suffered the loss of loved ones at Port Arthur and that person concluded the letter I received in this term "I can but keep surviving to enshrine their spirit in the world. The incredible unconditional love, the warmth and freedom, the laughter, the dances, the spontaneity, cuddling and kissing, they are no longer there. I will, however, proudly endeavour to keep their spirits alive throughout my life. My love for them will never die and can never be taken."

"And that is a response which many people who suffered the loss of loved ones have expressed to me as well, I might say," Mr Bugg told the court.

This incisive presentation showed clearly what impact the Port Arthur massacre had had on not only those directly involved but the wider community in general.

All through Mr Bugg's presentation, Martin Bryant sat quietly in the dock, still surrounded by security guards and separated from the body of the court by the bullet proof glass panel, seemingly oblivious to what was being said.

During both days of the trial and then at the sentencing, there was no real indication from Bryant that he had any real interest in the proceedings at all. From what I saw, he didn't even take any interest in the Crown's submission on the background of Martin Bryant.

Mr Bugg put a great deal of information about Bryant before the court, but the most significant in the eyes of the media, was about his ability to be placed on trial at all.

He presented a report prepared by Hobart psychiatrist, Dr Ian Sale, which showed why Bryant did not attempt to enter an insanity plea.

"Your Honour, I refer you to the rest of the report now of Dr Sale which was obviously prepared by him at my request to determine whether or not Section 16 of our Criminal Code provided any explanation for Bryant's criminal responsibility.

"In other words was Bryant criminally insane at the time he committed these acts, and you will see that Dr Sale's conclusion was that there was no such defence available to him. He concluded that it was his opinion that the syndrome or disorder which explained much of the conduct that Bryant went through, which many people found either disconcerting and anti social or inappropriate was attributable to a syndrome called Asperger's Syndrome."

Dr Sale said that many of the indicia of that syndrome may

be said to be consistent with aspects of his (Bryant's) conduct or behaviour about which some comment or evidence had been given.

But he says these various indicia are just that, syndromes, constellations of behavioural patterns that are found together. There is no indication on causation which for all these syndromes remains speculative. What seems clear is that abnormalities were evident from Bryant's earliest days. He was likely born with these problems rather than acquiring them through an abnormal family environment.

Dr Sale's report also dealt with the early suggestions of Bryant being schizophrenic.

"The question of this man suffering from schizophrenia was the subject of some speculation but if I can take your Honour to the relevant section of Dr Sale's report.

"There is no form of mental illness, as the term is usually understood. He certainly does not manifest any psychotic illness such as schizophrenia. Personality disorder is generally subdivided into particularly commonly occurring patterns. Bryant does not fit into many of these sub types, they are obviously anti social traits, but he is not typical of individuals with this pattern of behaviour. Perhaps fortunately, he may be unique.

"I am confident that notwithstanding his disabilities, Bryant knows what he has been doing and can discern between right and wrong. Perhaps the clearest indicator of this is his maintaining a false account of the day in question, an account that is invented. There would be no need to invent this if he

were not aware of the wrongness of the behaviours for which he stands accused," Dr Sale wrote.

"Finally, I do not believe that he was acting under an irresistible impulse. His preparation for the day, taking firearms, petrol, handcuffs, getting up early, argue that at least some of the events of the day were planned ahead. His preparation for the day and the evidence that he was at Seascape before going to the Historic Site suggests that his major intention was to kill or harm the Martins and perhaps burn Seascape.

"Why he proceeded on a homicidal spree remains a mystery. He had previously caused concern during childhood when he shot birds or took potshots at tourists with his air rifle. His acquisition of military firearms and associated literature suggests that he may have held fantasies regarding their use. Other than occasional target practice he had no obvious other use nor did he associate with other gun users. Perhaps after he started at Seascape he succumbed to a previously held fantasy and took pot shots at tourists, only this time with lethal fire power at his disposal, rather than an air rifle.

"Unfortunately this remains speculation. Only he knows why he travelled to Port Arthur on 28th April and for the present he chooses not to reveal this" Dr Sale concluded.

At the time he made this report, Dr Sale was of the opinion that as for Bryant's prognosis, there would be no improvement on the condition.

Mr Bugg then went on to introduce an updated report on Bryant which was delivered to him on 13 November, 1996.

"I am now firmer in a conclusion that Bryant likely manifests a condition termed Asperger's Disorder, a developmental condition bearing some similarities to autism.

"From early on, childhood and cognitive development have been consistently abnormal. There have been problems with language and communication and especially with his social behaviour. In addition he has also been noted to have an unusual high voice, high pitched with little tonal variation and there are unusual mannerisms and motor behaviours.

"His affect whatever the circumstances appears fatuous and inappropriate. This was particularly evident during the recent court hearing (when he laughed during the pleas regarding the killing of the Mikac children). However, it should be noted that this type of behaviour appears to be the norm for Bryant. There is little variation. He appears to be incapable of experiencing or expressing empathy, remorse or guilt, those emotions which tend to act as brakes on social behaviour.

"Indeed his social behaviour has been frequently observed to be dis-inhibited, inappropriate and lacking in commonsense. The original description of Asperger's Disorder in 1994 referred to a lack of interpersonal empathy, solitariness and the pursuit of idiosyncratic goals. The patients show abnormalities of gaze, quality of expression and gesture and had unusual voice production. Whilst most individuals with Asperger's Disorder, going on from that last quotation are quiet, introverted and *present no hazard to the community there have been occasional other reports where violence has occurred although not of this scope.*

"Asperger's Disorder is not rare, probably occurring in approximately point three percent of the population. It is far more common in males. The cause is unknown although a genetic aetiology has been suggested. There is no evidence to suggest that an abnormal family environment plays a causative role.

"Indeed in this particular instance it would appear that his family have also been victims of his behaviour, albeit in a different way and over a protracted period. There is no treatment for the disorder which can be regarded as lifelong" Dr Sale concluded.

The Director of Public Prosecutions, after two solid days of presenting the Crown case against Martin Bryant ended simply,

"Your Honour, in conclusion I would make the submission I foreshadowed on the first day of these proceedings in relation to the sentencing of this young man. The position is clearly one where he is criminally responsible for his acts".

Mr Justice Cox then invited Bryant's lawyer, John Avery to begin his submissions.

After what the court had heard in the previous day and a half, Avery's job was not an easy one and as pitiable a case as he could present for Bryant, there were few in the court room that day that were prepared to even consider pity for him.

But Mr Avery did present what would be normally considered a plea in mitigation.

> "Your Honour, nothing that I can say on behalf of my client can mitigate the outrageous nature of his conduct. My learned friend has used highly charged language to describe the behaviour of Bryant over the course of this fateful day and I do not disagree at all with his description of this as a slaughter. The gross nature of the conduct defies logic or sane explanation and I am specifically instructed to make no submissions or place before the court any explanation or reason for this massacre other than can be gleaned from the medical material.
>
> "The reason and the answer to the burning question why must, at least for the time being, remain with the accused. All I can do is share with the court and the community the benefit of the expert material that has been obtained by the defence and try and give an insight into the mind of this man" Mr Avery told the court.

He went on to build his case around psychiatric reports into his client – the picture they revealed was, as Mr Justice Cox was to point out the next day, that of a pathetic individual.

Mr Avery started by citing a report from South Australian consultant psychiatrist, Dr William Lucas, who examined Bryant in prison on 12 May, 1996, and concluded that it was likely that he was suffering from a major psychiatric disorder.

He also stated a diagnosis of schizophrenia could not be made out on the basis of his examination. Dr Lucas had commented that Bryant has some unusual symptoms, but added that "I think it will turn out that this can be explained on the basis of a personality disorder combined with longstanding feelings of depression, rejection and alienation".

Dr Lucas however, also concluded Bryant was fit to plead at his trial, although would require some assistance in understanding his full legal situation and what is required of him.

Next Mr Avery turned to forensic psychologist, Mr Ian Joblin of Melbourne, who had interviewed Bryant twice and also carried out intelligence testing.

Under the verbal section, Bryant's IQ was calculated at 64. His performance in IQ testing was calculated at 72, giving a full scale IQ of 66.

Two other specific intelligence tests were conducted. The Ravens Coloured Progressive Matrices, which assesses the degree to which a person is able to think clearly saw Bryant score for Australian norms at a figure just greater than that which would be expected of an 11 year old child. The results indicated that if compared with a group of 11 year olds, 90 percent of these children would score higher than him on this test.

To complement that test, Mr Joblin also had Bryant undergo the Standard Progressive Matrices test which provides a measure of fluid intelligence eductive ability which is relatively independent of specific learning acquired in a particular cultural or educational context. This revealed an IQ figure for Bryant of 68, placing him in the second percentile, that is, relative to persons of his age group, 98 per cent would score higher than he did.

A further test of receptive vocabulary was also administered and Bryant who was 29 years and 24 days old at the time, scored an age equivalent of a child of 10 years and nine months old.

Mr Avery however, told the court that the opinion upon which the defence placed most reliance was that of Professor P.E.Mullen, a forensic psychiatrist from Victoria who examined all the material available about Bryant.

While he too concluded that a plea of insanity was not available as a defence, he did delve specifically into Bryant's family background.

"Mr Bryant is the eldest of two children, his father died three years ago and was described by the accused as a nice friendly quiet man with whom he had a good relationship. He was aware that his father had killed himself and agreed that his father had been down before the suicide.

"Mr Bryant was not able to give a description of his mother other than as someone who washed his clothes and cooked his food. Despite this, he considered himself to have a good relationship with her.

"Mr Bryant was more forthcoming about his younger sister, now aged 23, and who lives in Western Australia and works as a cook. He said that as children he found her difficult because she was much brighter than he and seemed to have lots of friends whereas he was painfully aware of the lack of such companions. He said though he was jealous of her as a kid their relationship greatly improved when she did so much to look after him following his road traffic accident in 1992.

"It was difficult to obtain any sense of the family environment from Mr Bryant's account other than his bland assessment that it was 'good', 'okay' and 'nice'.

"Mr Bryant's memories of school are that he found it an

unpleasant and distressing experience for virtually the whole of his attendance. He recalls frequently being bullied, he said 'I was hazed and knocked around all the time, no one wanted to be my friend'. He only recalls one companion at school and this was for a relatively brief period during childhood. The predominant memory is of being by himself, ignored by other children or attended to in a bullying or frightening manner" Professor Mullen wrote.

The tension in the courtroom while Mr Avery was presenting his submission remained almost touchable. The room was still full, no one was leaving, Bryant was still in the dock and the Port Arthur people continued staring at him and trying to comprehend the plea in mitigation being put to the court.

Outside, Court 8 was also still packed with media and some police and court officials who were keen to hear what was unfolding next door.

The prize for the faux pas of the entire trial has to be awarded to Mr Avery. At one stage he was reading from notes about things that had been written about Bryant.

The particular problem arose when he began reading this passage; "he (Bryant) described his pleasure in life as watching television, music and killing." – sorry, I'll re-read that. "Mr Bryant described his pleasure in life as watching the television and music and drinking. The music that he most favoured was the sound track of the Lion King and records made by Cliff Richard."

Given the nature of the trial there was no spontaneous gasp or laughter from the people in the court, and I think that reflected the strain that all involved in the case were feeling.

Another quirk to emerge that day was a claim by the

defence that Bryant had never acquired a gun licence, partly because he was afraid of the difficulty answering questions about safe gun usage.

The court was also told that afternoon of Bryant's mental state which was ascertained from extensive interviews with him after April 28th.

Professor Mullen said Bryant had tried to live day by day but acknowledges that frequently, thoughts about past rejections and what he recalls as his victimisation at school by bullies intrudes. He has become more caught up in these thoughts about past indignities over the last year. He said he had become increasingly unhappy and angry because he had no real friend. He said, "all I wanted was for people to like me", their failure to respond to his overtures led him to feel that "I'd had a gut full".

The professor said "This culminated in the month before the tragedy in a sense that there was no future for him, that he would always remain lonely and rejected and that he would be better off dead. Bryant said 'about 12 months ago I decided I'd had enough, the thoughts of suicide became more prominent in recent months'.

"He also became more caught up in ruminating on memories of slights and insults of the past and he began to think about these things a great deal and began to go over in his mind how he could get even.

"Initially he said he thought about strangling someone who was unfriendly to him, but then his thoughts turned to shooting him. Mr Bryant said 'I thought guns would be better, the more power the better'."

He stated to Professor Mullen he was unsure exactly when

the plan came to him for the massacre at Port Arthur. He said that "he thought the plan first occurred to him a few weeks prior to the tragic events". When pressed he thought it might have been four, or as long as twelve weeks that this first occurred.

When asked why he selected Port Arthur he responded "a lot of violence has happened there. It must be the most violent place in Australia. It seemed the right place".

Bryant also spoke of his long standing resentment against Mr and Mrs Martin. He described them as very mean people "as the worst people in my life". The basis for this antipathy appears to be Mr Bryant's belief that Mr Martin bought the property which they occupied at their death (Seascape) with the expressed intention of preventing his father from buying the same property.

Mr Avery then interposed to clarify an issue which had become almost fact in Tasmania since the shootings. He told the court that Bryant had asked him to correct the point put by Mr Bugg that it was the Seascape property that was the centre of any dispute.

"Indeed it was the property, the farm, the Larner property, that my client believes was the property his father wanted to buy and not the Seascape property" Mr Avery said.

Professor Mullen's report went on "Mr Bryant assumed that when he began shooting at Port Arthur he would himself be shot down. He stated in one interview, "My power, so powerful and the guns and these magazines filled with bullets, I could just go bang, bang, bang".

"This plan to kill Mr and Mrs Martin and then proceed to Port Arthur appears initially to have been elaborated following the breakup of a relationship at a time when he was particularly despondent about his situation and his future.

"Although with the initiation of the relationship with Miss Wilmot, his mood improved and his suicidal pre-occupation disappeared, nonetheless this dreadful plan appears to have been persisted with and eventually to have been put into awful practice. I did not pursue with Mr Bryant any account of the actual killings, as these can sadly be all too readily reconstructed from eye witness accounts and police investigations".

Professor Mullen said "the enormity of Mr Bryant's crimes call out for some explanation equally dramatic and extraordinary. It is not to be wondered at that the media have either attempted to portray Mr Bryant as afflicted by a dramatic mental illness, such as schizophrenia, or to be some kind of evil genius.

"In my opinion, the origins of this terrible tragedy are not to be found in a simple, dramatic and sufficient cause, but in the interaction and combination of a range of influences and events. We may never know fully the intentions and state of mind which led to the killings.

"There also has to be acknowledgment that Mr Bryant took delight and gained excitement from tormenting others. This reaction of the frightened child to their own sense of powerlessness emerged in the adult as the desire to assert himself through the killing and maiming of others. He was an individual capable of taking delight not only in the fantasies of such destruction but in the event to delight in acting out these dreadful daydreams.

"There is in Mr Bryant an apparent sense of guilt, albeit truncated, about his actions, but equally on occasion he almost revels in the memory of his awful day, awful acts."

Professor Mullen ended his report "Mr Bryant currently

does not have the signs and symptoms of a mental illness. He is however, by virtue of his personality and intellectual limitations both of reduced coping ability and of increased psychological vulnerability.

"It is possible that under the combined stress of lengthy incarceration of having to live with the memories and consequences of his awful acts that they may in the future break down into frank mental illness. It will be necessary to continually monitor his state of mind during his future containment and initiate appropriate treatment as and when required".

Mr Avery then addressed the court. "Your Honour, that is the report that I will tender to the court. Your Honour, what therefore do we say is the totality of the medical evidence concerning that of Dr Sale. Firstly it is abundantly clear that at the time of the commission of these crimes and at the present day the accused is not criminally insane.

"Secondly, although it has been thought in his early years that perhaps he suffered schizophrenia, it can now conclusively be claimed that there is no evidence to support the notion that this man has a schizophrenic illness.

"Thirdly, it appears that the accused does not fit into any neat pigeon hole of particular mental illness.

"Fourthly, he clearly is intellectually disabled and without the support of his father and Miss Harvey and with the access to funds he regrettably found himself able, with ferocious consequence to carry out this mass destruction.

"Finally your Honour, it would be apparent the accused revels in the notoriety he has achieved but in his simple way accepts the enormity of his actions and as a result has instructed me to comment on penalty.

"Your Honour, Martin Bryant accepts that in all probability he will never be released from prison and will die there. He also accepts that that would not be an inappropriate penalty" Mr Avery said.

There followed some short legal debate about the indictment against Bryant and suddenly the trial of the man who killed thirty-five people at Port Arthur and caused untold suffering to entire communities, was over.

From the bench, Mr Justice Cox said "the prisoner is remanded for sentence until 10 am on Friday, (the next day) let him stand down".

Bryant was taken from the court for the trip back to Risdon Prison; and the media had another day of being overloaded with information which they would try to condense for the public in their news bulletins and current affairs programs that night and the newspapers the next day.

I had an interesting incident at the end of this day's hearings. During the lunch break I had seen Ray Martin of the *Nine Network* arrive at the court. He was mingling with the other media crews and obviously had come down to finalise a program on Port Arthur.

In the corridor I met Wendy Scurr, who was one of those who gave medical assistance at Port Arthur on the day and who has suffered since the incident. She asked if I knew Ray and I said only by reputation, but I had spoken to him a little earlier in my role as media officer, and so she asked if I could introduce her because she would love to meet him.

She said she had appeared in an interview program with him,

where he asked the questions, but said she had never spoken to him. I asked how did that happen, and she said "well someone else had asked her the questions and then when the program appeared it was Ray Martin asking the questions". Wendy thought television was very clever to be able to do that. Wendy's story, not mine. I also thought it was very clever, but not surprising.

Martin Bryant was to be sentenced for his crimes at 10 am on Friday 22nd, November, 1996.

THE SENTENCING OF MARTIN BRYANT

With sentencing to proceed the next day, the media decided they would like to broadcast the event live on radio and television. They could see great public interest in such a broadcast and approaches were made both to me and the Court.

The person with the ultimate say in such matters was the Chief Justice. The answer that came back was the same as it had been before the start of the trial. There would be no live broadcast.

And it was the media's own fault; let me point out why.

Had the original approach, at least the one I knew of, not been so ham fisted and legally naive, there may well have been direct broadcasting of the proceedings. However, that approach left the judge with no alternative but to decline.

From a television news director came a letter dated 3 October, 1996, to the Chief Justice which began; "I write with a special request to televise live to air your sentencing in the Martin Bryant trial."

Now bear in mind here that even Martin Bryant was entitled to the presumption of innocence until proven guilty.

But the letter gets worse; "It would be greatly appreciated if you could give due consideration to the televising live of your sentencing and reasons, following the jury's verdict. As there is great public interest involved, the fact that this incredible crime affected almost everyone in Tasmania in some way, and the wider implications of gun control nationally, I am sure that your considered judgement broadcast live to air without editing would not only be vital to all Tasmanians, but historically of national interest and significance. Your decision may also have a bearing on the healing process so important to us all.

"Unique as the request is, I feel it's important for everyone in Tasmania to have the opportunity to witness live your sentencing and considered views of Martin Bryant. I would appreciate further discussion on the proposal if you deem it worthwhile."

I don't think this person did appreciate what little further discussion there was on the issue. The answer was no and you can all probably see why.

How would it look for the Chief Justice to have agreed even before a trial had started, to allow live televising of his 'sentencing'? Sometimes those in the media with little expertise in the law, or indeed a scant regard for it, are their own worst enemies.

And so it was that shortly after 10 am on 22nd November, 1996, Mr Justice Cox delivered the following address to a packed Court 7 in the Supreme Court complex in Hobart.

"In consequence of the tragic events at Port Arthur on 28/29 April this year and of this plea of guilty to the unprecedented list of crimes contained in the indictment before me, the

prisoner stands for sentence in respect of the murder of no less than thirty-five persons; of twenty attempts to murder others; of the infliction of grievous bodily harm on yet three more; and of the infliction of wounds upon a further eight persons.

"In addition, he is to be sentenced for four counts of aggravated assault; one count of unlawfully setting fire to property, namely a motor vehicle which he seized at gunpoint from its rightful occupants, all of whom he murdered; and for the arson of a building known as Seascape, the owners of which he had likewise murdered the previous day.

"After having heard the unchallenged account of these terrible events narrated by the learned Director of Public Prosecutions and his Junior, an account painstakingly prepared by them from the materials diligently assembled by the team of police and forensic investigators charged with the task, it is unnecessary for me to repeat it in detail or to attempt more than a brief summary.

"The prisoner, it is clear, a lengthy period of time before the day on which it was carried into effect, formed the intention of causing the deaths of Mr and Mrs Martin against whom he had long harboured a grudge and at the very least of causing mayhem among the large group of residents and visitors he anticipated would be present at the Port Arthur historic site, by shooting at them. Indeed he seems to have contemplated mayhem of such a drastic kind that it would in all probability provoke a response which would result in his own death.

"In furtherance of his intention, he acquired high powered weapons and embarked with three of them, a very large supply of ammunition and accessories such as a sports bag to conceal

the weapons, a hunting knife, two sets of handcuffs and rope. In addition, he carried large quantities of petrol in containers, fire starters and acquired a cigarette lighter en route. As he was not a smoker, the inference is that he intended to arm himself with the means of igniting the petrol and that this was intended to be used in unlawfully causing damage to some property in the course of his expedition.

"Arriving at the Martins' home, he shot both of them dead and continued on to Port Arthur. There at the Broad Arrow Cafe, he consumed a meal on the balcony outside and then, re-entering the cafe, placed the bag on an unoccupied table. He produced from the bag an AR15 rifle fitted with a 30 shot magazine and commenced to fire at close range at patrons who were complete strangers to him. In the first 15 seconds he discharged 17 rounds, thereby causing the deaths of twelve people, the infliction of grievous bodily harm to a thirteenth, wounds to five more, and injuries to an additional four whom he attempted unsuccessfully to murder.

"Moving through the cafe to the gift shop annexed to it, he continued to discharge the weapon at close quarters before leaving the premises approximately one and a half minutes (90 seconds) after firing the first shot. In that period of 90 seconds, 29 rounds were fired causing the deaths of twenty people and injuries, many of them severe, to another twelve who fortunately escaped with their lives.

"In addition, the spectators who escaped physical injury were subjected to emotional trauma of the most stressful kind. Although not the subject of any count in the indictment, this form of injury was clearly a by-product of the prisoner's wrongful conduct.

"In the cafe he changed magazines and leaving it, he fired indiscriminately at various parts of the historic site intending to hit and kill those who were within range. In the car park, where there were a number of buses, he shot the driver of one in the back, killing him, and fired at groups of people seeking shelter in them or in their vicinity. Here he killed another person and caused injuries to a further three.

"He then exchanged the Armalite rifle for a semi automatic .308 FN rifle, or SLR which was in the boot of his car parked nearby and fired across the water towards the ruins and back towards the cafe. Still in the car park, the prisoner killed two further visitors and by firing shots which, in some cases, connected, attempted to murder six others.

"From here he moved up the road in his car and en route encountered Mrs Mikac and her two daughters, murdering all three in the heart rending circumstances already described by the Director of Public Prosecutions.

"At the toll booth he murdered the four occupants of a BMW, pulling the two female passengers seated in it from the car and shooting them at close range. He then commandeered the car, transferring from his own car some of the items in it, including the AR15 rifle, a quantity of ammunition, the two handcuffs and some petrol. Thereafter he fired two shots at a car which had been reversed by the driver on appreciating the situation. In the vicinity of the toll booth, eleven spent cartridges fired by the prisoner were later recovered.

"A short distance from the toll booth a white Corolla occupied by Mr Glen Pears and Miss Zoe Hall was parked at the service station. The prisoner brought the vehicle he was driving to a halt on the wrong side of the road and blocked the passage of the Corolla. He alighted with the SLR and tried to extract Miss Hall from the passenger seat. When Mr Pears attempted to intervene, he was forced into the boot of the prisoner's stolen vehicle. Miss Hall was then murdered in a series of three rapid shots from the hip and the prisoner moved on, returning to Seascape.

"On the way, and after his arrival, he fired at a number of vehicles causing very grievous harm to the occupant of one of them and endangering the lives of nine other people, including two police officers called to the scene.

"Arrived at Seascape the prisoner forced Mr Pears, whom he was treating as a hostage, to enter the house, placed handcuffs on his wrists and immobilised him by attaching a second set of handcuffs to the first and some fixture in the premises. He then set fire to the stolen vehicle and retreated into the house, where at some time before his apprehension, he murdered Mr Pears by shooting him.

"Throughout the night he continued to discharge a number of weapons, his own arsenal augmented by weapons belonging to the Martins, and kept at bay by police who were surrounding the house, their response restricted by the belief that both the Martins and Mr Pears could still be alive. Clearly the Martins were not alive at that stage, but the prisoner deceitfully conveyed the impression they were in telephone conversations with police negotiators. The following morning he set fire to the house, destroying it completely and, while fleeing from it in an injured condition due to burns, was apprehended.

"Objectively, it is difficult to imagine a more chilling catalogue of crime. The prisoner, having had a murderous plan in contemplation and active preparation for some time, deliberately killed two persons against whom he held a grudge, and then embarked on a trail of devastation which took the lives of a further thirty-three human beings who were total strangers to him and which caused serious injury, distress and grief to literally thousands more. The repercussions of these crimes have been world-wide.

"His selection of victims was indiscriminate. He killed and injured men, women and even children. He killed or attempted to kill, local residents, visitors from other parts of the State, from other parts of Australia and visitors from a number of overseas countries. He killed individual family members, married couples and in one case, all the members of one family save the bereaved father left to mourn them.

"The learned Director of Public Prosecutions has mentioned the impact these crimes have had on individuals immediately affected by the loss of a family member or members, or who have suffered physical injury in the course of this shocking rampage. He has also mentioned the effect it had on eye witnesses who experienced the nightmare as it ran its course or who came upon the scene or otherwise had to cope with the injured and dead.

"This is not the place to acknowledge the contributions made by groups or individuals in dealing with the aftermath of these crimes. No doubt they will be acknowledged elsewhere. Suffice it to say that there were many, many people who were severely affected by their distressing experiences and who will

continue to be so affected for many years to come. It is proper to record also the anguish no doubt caused to the prisoner's mother and immediate family.

"Then there is the effect on the community at large: the shock and disbelief that criminal conduct on this scale could occur in Australia, let alone Tasmania; the feelings of outrage, anger, grief and frustration at not being able to do more to redress the wrong suffered by so many innocent victims.

"Though in no way comparable to the human suffering endured by those directly affected, very considerable financial loss has also been occasioned to individuals and to the community at large. In the sentencing process, the impact upon the victims of crime cannot be ignored. In this case more than any other I have ever experienced, they demand recognition.

"In determining an appropriate punishment the Court is required to have regard to many factors: the gravity of the offence or offences; the moral culpability of the offender so far as that lies within the limited province of human assessment; the effect upon the victims; the need to protect society from similar conduct by others, or repetition of it by the offender himself; his background and antecedents; any contrition or remorse on his part, and a host of other considerations.

"In the forefront of this case is the prisoner's mental condition. The law recognises that if a person is afflicted by a mental disease to such an extent that he is unable to understand the physical character of what he is doing in, for example, firing a weapon at another person, or that he is rendered incapable of knowing that such an act is one which he ought not to do, or if he acts under an impulse which, by

reason of mental disease, he is in substance deprived of any power to resist, then the person should not be held criminally responsible for an act which, in a sane person, would clearly amount to a crime. Society is entitled to be protected from such a person, but he may not be held criminally responsible.

"That great Australian jurist, Sir Owen Dixon, once observed that it was perfectly useless for the law to attempt, by threatening punishment, to deter people from committing crimes if their mental condition is such that they cannot be in the least influenced by the possibility or probability of subsequent punishment; if they cannot understand what they are doing or cannot understand the ground upon which the law proceeds. There is no utility, he said, in punishing people if they are beyond the control of the law for reasons of mental health.

"Nevertheless, a great number of people who come into a criminal court are abnormal. They would not be there if they were the normal type of average, everyday person. Many of them, he said, are very peculiar in their dispositions, but are mentally quite able to appreciate what they are doing and quite able to appreciate the threatened punishment of the law and the wrongness of their acts and they are held in check by the prospect of punishment.

"It is clear on the materials before me that the prisoner falls into the latter category. He is not suffering from a mental illness – certainly not one which rendered him incapable of knowing what he was doing or of knowing that what he was doing was wrong, or one by virtue of which he was deprived of any power to resist an impulse to do the things he did. He

knew what he was doing and that it was something he ought not to do.

"Nevertheless, he clearly has a mental condition which rendered him less capable than those of normal healthy mind of appreciating the enormity of his conduct or its effects upon others. I accept the psychiatric evidence that he is of limited intellectual ability, his measured IQ being in the borderline intellectually disabled range, but with a capacity to function reasonably well in the community. From an early age he has displayed severe developmental problems, being grossly disturbed from early childhood. Whatever its precise diagnosis as to which the psychiatrists differ, he suffers from a significant personality disorder.

"Professor Mullen said of him that his limited intellectual capacities and importantly his limited capacity for empathy or imagining the feelings and responses of others left a terrible gap in his sensibilities which enabled him not only to contemplate mass destruction, but to carry it through. Without minimising the gravity of his conduct or denying his responsibility for it, it would appear to me that the level of culpability is accordingly reduced by reason of his intellectual impairment and the disorder with which he has been afflicted for so long, notwithstanding his parents' earnest endeavours to correct it, which the medical records acknowledge. That the prisoner, through these handicaps, in combination with a number of external factors beyond his control such as the loss of stabilising influences, has developed into a pathetic social misfit calls for understanding and pity, even though his actions demand condemnation.

"The prisoner has shown no remorse for his actions. Though he has ultimately pleaded guilty, it has clearly been done in recognition of the undoubted strength of the evidence against him and amounts to little more than a bowing to the inevitable.

"That his change of plea has saved considerable distress, inconvenience and cost to those who would have been called as witnesses and to the victims and community at large by the prolongation of the proceedings is a factor which should be considered in his favour when weighing all the relevant considerations, but in the overall scheme of things, it is, in my view, overwhelmingly outweighed by the factors militating against him.

"Having regard to the nature and extent of his conduct, I cannot regard it as anything other than falling within the worst category of cases for which the maximum penalty is prescribed. Taking account of the medical evidence and his lack of insight into the magnitude and effect of his conduct apparent in all his appearances before this Court, I have no reason to hope and every reason to fear that he will remain indefinitely as disturbed and insensitive as he was when planning and executing the crimes of which he now stands convicted.

"The protection of the community, in my opinion, requires that he serve fully the sentences which I will shortly impose. That consideration, as well as my belief that service of the whole of such sentence is the minimum period of imprisonment which justice requires that he must serve having regard to all the circumstances of his offences leads to the conclusion that he should be declared ineligible for parole.

"*Martin Bryant – on each of the thirty-five counts of murder in the indictment you are sentenced to imprisonment for the term of your natural life.*

"*I order that you not be eligible for parole in respect of any such sentence. On each of the remaining counts in the indictment, you are sentenced to imprisonment for 21 years to be served concurrently with each other and with the concurrent sentences of life imprisonment already imposed. In respect to each sentence of 21 years, I order you likewise not be eligible for parole*".

Mr Justice Cox then ordered that Bryant be taken away. And he was.

There was a clear feeling of relief in the court – but it was mixed with emotional thoughts for those who had suffered at the hands of the person who had just been removed from the court, never to be seen in public again.

For a few seconds after Mr Cox left the chamber, no one moved, and then gradually the court began to empty. There was a feeling amongst many that it was finally over.

The Port Arthur people went back to the room provided for them to decide how they would leave the court, and if some or any would be prepared to speak to the media.

I had the job of trying to work out what was going to happen and then try to facilitate the best outcome for everyone.

With Bryant now sentenced there was going to be a mad scramble by the news crews to get hold of 'talent' to talk about Port Arthur and their own personal experiences.

While all this was happening, Mr Justice Cox had a surprise

of his own. I was called aside by Mr Bugg, the DPP, and handed an audio tape.

The Chief Justice, while not prepared to turn his sentencing into a media event on television for reasons already outlined, had shrewdly organised to have his address recorded, and then was considerate enough towards the media to have it released for use.

Radio was probably the most pleased, television seemed reasonably happy, but some still complained that they would rather have had pictures, which I think showed a complete lack of understanding at what had just happened.

Television seems to have the opinion that everything should happen for them – sometimes, such as this Supreme Court sentencing, they don't. And it was the fault of television.

The Port Arthur people mostly decided they would not talk to the media as they left the court complex but that there would be a news conference later in the day at which some of them would be available for questions.

I dutifully went out to the assembled media and tried to explain that what would happen would be that the Port Arthur people would leave the court complex in small groups and that very few were prepared to answer questions.

Given that these were the ground rules the Port Arthur people wanted, the media was happy enough, but then like the best laid plans of mice and men, the wheels very soon fell off the arrangements.

Those who were most opposed to talking to the media left first – and what did they do? They walked towards the media and had the obligatory questions put to them; and they stopped and talked, and talked and talked. I don't know why that happened, was underway during the second week in May, the questioning was still focussing on how the tragedy happened; and how sad it was to have happened in Tasmania, and how tragic it was to have happened in Port Arthur, and how beautiful and peaceful the State was.

Tasmanians had been bombarded mercilessly by the media in the first couple of days after Port Arthur and within a week or so had had enough and wanted to move on. And the local media recognised this. This is not a criticism of the local media because after all it was arguably the biggest story ever in Tasmania and the local media wanted to ensure their readers and viewers and listeners were fully informed. That was the major difference I noticed during the mission with Rundle, Noye and Mazengarb. From Melbourne we travelled to Ballarat where it had been arranged that the official party would meet several of the Howard children, whose parents Merv and Mary from Dunnstown had died at Port Arthur.

The meeting was organised for the Town Hall in the Mayor's office and it was probably the most emotionally crippling event I have ever been involved with.

What was there to say? The children had tragically lost their parents and nothing could be done to bring them back. It was stilted, for a start, with the main topic being football because no one really wanted to; or knew how best, to raise the subject of Port Arthur. Eventually, there were tears and questions without answers.

But that was when Neil Noye, whom I have described almost since the first days of the Port Arthur incident, as everybody's grandfather, came to the fore. His gentle manner saw him take to that end he embarked on a week-long mission around the mainland with both the Mayor of Tasman, Neil Noye and chairman of the Port Arthur Historic Site, Michael Mazengarb. The idea was, in effect, to convey the thanks of Tasmanians to the other states who offered help and support throughout the tragedy. It was also to ask, indeed plead with them, not to now turn their backs on the State as far as a tourist destination was concerned.

The Premier was criticised in some areas for making the trip – but he really had no alternative.

Rundle and the others took with them open letters from the people of the Tasman Peninsula asking that fellow Australians come and visit the State and their particular area and to talk to them. The mission was to back their resolve that the State needed to quickly return to normal and that the best thing people could do was not turn away now.

It was a tortuous timetable which took us from Hobart to Melbourne, Ballarat, Canberra, Sydney, Brisbane, Adelaide and back to Hobart all in a week.

Rundle, Noye and Mazengarb took in all the media opportunities that presented themselves and Rundle in particular, was impressive in his commitment and enthusiasm to do what was needed to get the message across.

But while the media were supportive of Tasmania and wanted to do what they could to help our situation, I think the mainland actually took longer to start moving on from the tragedy than most Tasmanians did.

Interestingly from my estimation, the mainland trailed by about two weeks. And by this I mean that when the mainland tour but it overturned all the planning that had gone into "protecting" them as they left the building.

The assembled media was happy enough because it gave them more new copy, and it probably did the Port Arthur people some good as well, because some of them got a lot off their chests.

It was as I walked up Salamanca Place with a small group of survivors that I came unstuck for the first and only time during the Port Arthur incident.

I was walking with Carolyn Loughton, who was very severely wounded by Bryant during his rampage in the Broad Arrow Cafe and indeed had lost her 15 year old daughter during the shooting. Carolyn had been suffering badly ever since 28 April, and the trial and reliving it all again, had seen her condition go backwards. After the sentencing she was set to erupt, and later that day she did.

As we walked she put her arm around me and started crying, saying "I have nothing, I have lost everything" (meaning her daughter), and she said she "thought even the death penalty for Bryant was too good for him".

It was heart wrenching stuff – I really didn't know what to do. I left them in the room that had been provided for them daily during the trial and sentencing by the Department of Community and Health Services and went back to the court complex.

I was met by Norm Beaman from *Network Ten* and I don't know what he said, but I broke down and burst into tears. I couldn't help it. Carolyn Loughton was right, she had lost everything in the world that mattered to her, and Bryant (in her estimation) was simply put in prison.

It didn't seem fair and I could understand her feelings at the time. As Norm and I stood on the court complex steps, I tried to explain this conversation with Carolyn to him and my eyes were streaming with tears. A television cameraman saw this and picked up his gear and was going to film whatever it was he saw happening.

Thankfully, Norm saw him moving and simply said, "He's one of ours, don't worry." And the camera was put down again. I will be forever grateful to Norm for that show of compassion, it may well have made a good 'side bar' to his story that night but he let it go. After a few minutes I was right again and it was back to work and reality.

My biggest disappointment with the media came at the end of the sentencing of Bryant.

All throughout the trial I had bent over backwards to provide the media with what they needed.

I took a television camera crew into the prison to get footage of Bryant's cell and the hospital etc. We also took in a newspaper photographer, Roger Lovell, to get the same shots for the print media so everyone was covered.

And even on this last day I had managed to persuade the authorities to allow a television camera and a newspaper photographer inside the prison at Risdon to film the prison van with Bryant, as it drove down the long internal drive to the Prison Hospital.

They weren't prepared to allow close up footage of Bryant but the cameras did get an image of him being ushered into the hospital. Under the circumstances, I thought everyone, from police to prison authorities to the Justice Department, had cooperated marvellously to help the media get what they needed, within the boundaries of reasonableness.

But still the media has this drive to get something different to everyone else, and what happened on this day could have been catastrophic.

Security is only security if it isn't known to everyone, and some of the sillier calls I received over Port Arthur were the ones who asked if we could tell them what security arrangements had been put in place to bring Bryant back and forward to the court from prison.

Please just think of it yourself for a moment; if everyone knows what arrangements have been made, why have security at all?

Anyway, on the day Bryant was sentenced, the media were not to know, but that doesn't change things. Police and prison officials had received a telephone warning in the morning that "something might happen".

The warning was in terms of telling the police and prison officers to "keep their heads down after the sentencing". While it was an anonymous threat, like several others that were received during that week, it was given more weight than the other calls because of some detailed knowledge the caller had of prison and police operations.

Bryant was transferred daily in a convoy and the essence of security for a convoy is speed and continual movement – the convoy should not stop or be slowed anywhere on its route from the prison to the court or back again. And on each day so far, it had worked that way without problems. But not this last day.

Would you believe that as the convoy was heading out of the City back to Risdon, a media team acted in a way which could easily have led to another disaster?

If there was to be a threat to the convoy, such as spraying the van with bullets, it could easily have been done as it entered onto the Tasman Bridge, and so it would be essential that nothing impede the progress of the convoy, especially on the Bridge.

However, on Bryant's last ride back to jail, just as the convoy hit the bridge and began the journey up the incline, a hired van pulled in front of it and slowed down. The rear door of the van was flung open, upwards, and a television cameraman was sitting in the back taking pictures of the police vehicles and the prison van going up the bridge.

The van driver slowed the entire convoy so his cameraman could get the pictures they obviously thought would 'scoop' all other networks.

As I said, they were not to know about the threats to the convoy that morning, but the slowing of such a convoy was an act of gross irresponsibility. What would have happened I wonder, had the police been a little bit nervous that day and taken some drastic and immediate action against this van, which was doing something which could in the circumstances, have easily have been considered as hostile.

Sergeant Nick Watchorn was in charge of security for the convoy. His men managed to get the van out of the way without any real incident, but he was fuming when he got back to the court complex.

He asked me who the crew were and I pointed them out to him. He spoke to the reporter who seemed beastly careless that he had caused any problems at all. The attitude he exhibited towards Nick was bordering on belligerence and 'how dare you tell me I nearly caused major problems because I am a network star just doing my job of informing the public' type thing.

Anyway, I had had enough by then and from my office called the producer of the program for which this person worked. The producer wasn't really interested in talking to me, so then I called the Managing Director of the television station.

I told him I had been in charge of the media liaison for the Bryant trial and that one of his crew had acted in a way which could easily have caused a major disaster with the convoy on the way back to the prison.

He, unlike the producer, was more than keen to hear what I had to say, and agreed that the action of slowing any such convoy was not appropriate, and offered to take it up with the reporter.

He asked if I wanted him to call back and let me know what the outcome of his probe into the incident was. I said no, I would leave it with him and heard nothing more about the incident. But I was interested to read in the national newspaper the next January that this particular person was one of three or four who had not had their contracts renewed by that network for 1997.

At 2 pm that afternoon the representatives of Port Arthur held a news conference at the Hobart Town Hall.

It was to involve people such as Neil Noye, the Mayor of Tasman, the Port Arthur Historic Site Management and staff from the site. It all went well enough until Carolyn Loughton, who had been sitting at the back of the room, decided she wanted to have something to say.

As I said earlier, Carolyn had been a dormant volcano all day simply waiting to erupt, and she did.

She took control of the conference as it was being closed, and launched a fairly strident attack on the Federal Government over its victim compensation arrangements.

Carolyn was very lucid and to the point, with what she wanted to say, and at one stage threatened to take off her blouse to show the media her horrific scars from the bullets fired into her by Bryant on 28th April.

And from the trial transcript let me remind you what Carolyn had been through; "Carol Loughton and her daughter Sarah who had been (in the Broad Arrow Cafe) with Mr Colyer (another victim of Bryant) were separated by a short distance but Sarah ran towards her mother and they both fell to the floor together, with Mrs Loughton covering her daughter. Mrs Loughton described the noise of the gun being discharged as very loud. She in fact has a ruptured eardrum caused by the explosion of that firearm. Whilst Mrs Loughton and her daughter were on the floor, Bryant shot Mrs Loughton in the back and shot Sarah in the head. It is most likely at this time that the close proximity of the shot to the back of Sarah's head caused the explosive noise which ruptured Mrs Loughton's eardrum.

"The injuries Mrs Loughton suffered were horrific. She sustained a wound to her back which was ten centimetres in diameter. She was evacuated by helicopter and did not know until she had been operated on and come out of surgery the next day that her daughter had been murdered" Damian Bugg told the trial.

And so who was going to step in and stop Carolyn having her say about anything she wanted to say? Certainly not me.

Because the conference was breaking up when she decided to speak her mind, I had been at the front of the room with

Neil Noye and ended up standing beside Carolyn. Nearby was a psychologist who had been working with Carolyn over the previous week or so, and I quietly asked what should I do, and he said "nothing, let her talk" so we did.

By this stage in the entire Port Arthur disaster, the television cameramen, the newspaper photographers and indeed the reporters had reached overload – the whole thing was just too consuming and emotionally they were as drained as everyone else who had been in anyway involved with the incident.

Carolyn made her statements and the packed media room listened politely, almost timidly. She was very emotional, but very powerful in the way she made her point. She then thanked the media for listening, and left.

I met her as she left the side entrance of the Town Hall and she grabbed my arm and said, "How did I go?"

I said "well thank heaven you left the State Government out of it, I thought we were in for a bashing there for a bit, and I was only going to stop you if you started taking your clothes off".

She laughed and said thanks for that. "Do you know where I work? I am a Commonwealth Public Servant," she said and laughed again. But this time compared to just a few hours ago, she sounded happy. I thought and indeed hoped that in some way she had lifted a huge emotional burden from herself that afternoon.

For me it was back to the office to await the Premier, who was travelling back from the north of the State to hold a news conference of his own on Port Arthur.

As usual, just before the Premier arrived I asked that all mobile phones be turned off because they have become a curse in recent years. They always ring at the most inopportune times.

Anyway the media assured me all phones were off and the Premier began his opening remarks about how Tasmania was now looking forward with Bryant locked away in prison for good.

Not a minute into his remarks, a phone rang. It belonged to a local freelance radio reporter who had not attended a conference of the Premier in the previous six months, but who was cashing in on Port Arthur and the Bryant trial by sending/selling reports to some mainland stations who didn't send their own reporters to Hobart.

I must admit I glared at her but said nothing as she left to take the call.

Rundle continued with the conference and was being hammered fairly hard on whether or not the death penalty should be reinstated in Australia. This could have been a ticklish question in any circumstance, but on a day when a man who kills thirty-five people is sentenced to life imprisonment, could have set a whole new debate raging in this country.

I admired his response which short circuited the questioning. He said that he was against the death penalty, and when asked why said "I had been in England in the 1960's when an innocent man had been put to death".

That ended the issue.

But just then there was a second call on a mobile phone, and would you believe it was the same one again. The woman had come back in and hadn't turned it off. This time, I was a little shorter with her and told her what I thought. She snapped back that, "she was a radio reporter and needed to keep her phone on at all time." I think I suggested something like she would never be a radio reporter, while ever her bum pointed to the earth, but was too tired and cranky to worry about it much more.

The Rundle conference ended and I went back to the office, but there was little more to do that day, and to be honest there was little more that I wanted to do.

By chance, I wandered down to the Customs House Hotel next to work to try to get a late lunch, where I ran into Damian Bugg, and a short time later Nick Perks, who just happened to be having a few drinks to celebrate what for them had been an entirely appropriate outcome.

Damian was just about in full flight, and enjoying it, and who can blame him. Nick was a little more subdued but then after a couple of drinks he relaxed and suddenly became very emotional.

Remember, he after all, was the one who had to deal with all the police forensic photographs from Port Arthur and the real horror of what happened while meticulously putting together the Crown case with Damian.

It was a moving incident and one which I felt privileged to be a small part of. He and Damian had done a tremendous job in ensuring that Bryant was not only locked away forever; but locked away before Christmas, just seven months after his murderous rampage. It was important to Tasmania that there be some symbolic line in the sand from which the community could move forward.

The work of the DPP and his team provided that line, and I don't know if the local community fully appreciated just how much work went into getting Bryant to court before the end of the year.

Meanwhile, the media who had been in Hobart covering the trial, got to hear that Damian may be at the Customs House Hotel (Hobart is a very small place), and as is their want, they started to turn up as well to rub shoulders with him and talk about the case.

It is one of the delights of Hobart that after such a momentous case as the Bryant trial, the media could turn up at a local hotel in the city and have a drink with the Crown Counsel and his junior, or rather; they could buy the Crown Counsel and his junior a drink.

The scene had all the hallmarks of turning into a long session of drinking and yarn spinning and whatever else journalists do when they have a night on the grog.

For my part, I was so knackered from a very busy week that after a couple of drinks with some former colleagues from radio in Sydney years earlier, I called it a day and went home and slept.

SOME REFLECTIONS

Once the trial was over, the media was free to print the stories they had been unable to do before Bryant's court appearances were finalised.

Four days after the sentencing, the *Hobart Mercury*, on 26 November, had a detailed account by Peter Mickelburough of the day seven months earlier, when Bryant went on his rampage.

"It's hard to imagine, but the death toll could have been much higher at Port Arthur if not for some good planning, many dedicated people and a little luck. Even before the final shots rang out, people were beginning the rescue attempt.

"Port Arthur security officer Ian Kingston, also Tasman Peninsula SES co-ordinator, was on the scene and as the killing began he quickly ushered several hundred people, all potential targets, to flee to safety. Another staff member, Wendy Scurr, a volunteer ambulance officer, made the first calls to the police and the ambulance brigade.

"In fact, 90% of those working at Port Arthur have first aid training and a number are volunteers with the *ambulance, fire or SES services. Those not wounded themselves quickly began to help.*

"'The early actions of Historic Site staff in triage, treatment and crowd control made a significant impact on the life chances of many of those who were injured,' Tasmanian Ambulance Service director, Grant Lennox said.

"Mr Lennox said Port Arthur had long been identified as a potential site for a multiple casualty incident, such as a bus crash, and so had been the scene of a number of disaster training exercises. This meant logistic questions such as travel times, locations of supplies and personnel were instantly available to those co-ordinating the response. Luck also lent a hand. Normally, Tasmania only has one rescue helicopter available, but that Sunday there were three choppers and pilots available.

"On the day of the massacre, the Royal Australian College of Surgeons was holding a course on early management of severe trauma for rural and other doctors. The Royal Hobart Hospital's directors of emergency medicine and surgery were both involved and immediately able to take charge, while those involved in the course were also deployed.

"Just two days before the shootings, the hospital had completed an eight month review of its emergency plans. So those responsible for the plan knew instantly the steps to follow when the shooting occurred. And just as luck would have it, in the week before the tragedy there had been a two day aviation emergency seminar in Hobart where issues including media management and community recovery had been examined.

"The helicopters were sent within minutes of the alarm being raised, taking with them six paramedics and supplies. At the same time, two ambulances and two ambulance station wagons left carrying another eight staff and more supplies. The first ambulance crew (a local unit from the Peninsula) reached the tollgate (at Port Arthur) within 14 minutes and shortly after, two local GPs and a volunteer unit, including two volunteers and an off-duty paramedic who lived in the area. Help was also given by bystanders including an off duty Hobart nurse and two interstate doctors visiting as tourists and an off duty NSW policeman.

"While Port Arthur is a 90 minute drive from Hobart, it is only 12-14 minutes by chopper. The first patient was flown from there at 2.56 pm, less than 1½ hours after the first shot had been fired. The critically wounded patient was accompanied only by a police officer as the ambulance crew could not leave the scene with so many still requiring treatment. Medical supplies and police were flown in on return journeys. Other critically wounded patients were flown out at 3.07, 3.40, 3.45, and 4.16. The remaining thirteen patients were transported by road in four ambulances and a bus which carried seven patients and two paramedics. The bus also carried some family members of the injured.

"The hospital's emergency department was first notified of the tragedy at 2.50. All emergency beds were made free before the first patient arrived and extra staff called in and theatres prepared. It was decided not to send a medical response team to Port Arthur given the level of experience of

those already on the scene. 'The hospital rapidly had in place eight fully staffed resuscitation teams and five fully staffed theatres ready to receive the first patients,' Mr Lennox said.

"'Many staff attended without being called in after hearing of the disaster and at one point there were forty-two doctors in the emergency area. The first patients arrived at 3.18; patients continued to arrive at regular intervals until 6.20 when the bus arrived.

"'Twenty-two patients were treated at the hospital, with four, including Martin Bryant, arriving the next day. In all, sixteen patients were admitted. Eleven operations were performed on the Sunday night, nine the next day and four later, with some patients having multiple surgery. Four patients were later sent to interstate hospitals by air ambulance.

"'One of the unique aspects of the hospital's role during the disaster was that it received all the patients, all the deceased, and the alleged gunman,' Mr Lennox said. This meant added pressure on hospital staff with community anger against Bryant directed at the hospital in a steady stream of abusive phone calls over the following days. Two bomb threats were made against the hospital and some hospital staff were accosted in the street for treating Bryant.

"Mr Lennox said the recovery strategy also started within 90 minutes of the first shots being fired when critical incident stress debriefing teams began the task of counselling the emergency personnel involved. Eight community counsellors were sent to the Tasman Peninsula on Sunday afternoon and a major counselling session was arranged at the Hobart Police Academy for relatives of the victims and witnesses. Twenty counsellors were involved in counselling 120 people there. Another twelve manned a police hotline on Sunday night to speak to relatives and friends of victims as they rang-in from across the state, country and overseas. Calls to the hotline averaged 48 minutes each. Counselling teams were also sent to two major Hobart hotels to assist affected tourists.

"Altogether, there were 463 staff from state and federal departments, non-government organisations and private practitioners involved in community recovery programs from the day of the shooting up until May 10. Of those, 408 had expertise in psychology, psychiatry, trauma or critical incident stress counselling. 'Tasmania's health team should be very proud of the manner in which they responded to the Port Arthur tragedy,' Mr Lennox said. 'Through their skilled efforts all those who were injured and not killed almost instantly at the scene are still alive today'".

I think that article wonderfully sums up the immediate response by the Tasmanian health team, and they deserve enormous credit for their work not only on 28th April, but over the following days and weeks.

It was now December; Christmas 1996 would soon be here – for me it had been an enormously long year.

A couple of days before Christmas, my wife and I were doing some last minute shopping at Myers in Hobart when my mobile phone rang.

It was a reporter from the *Herald Sun* in Melbourne who

wanted to know "what would Martin Bryant be having for Christmas Dinner this year?"

At first I thought it was a joke and asked them to repeat the question. They did – and at the end of a very long and difficult year, I had no patience left. I know the correct answer should have been "exactly what the other prisoners will get" but that wasn't what I said. "I don't give a fuck what Martin Bryant has for Christmas dinner this year, I know that no one in Tasmania gives a fuck and I don't think you should either" and basically terminated the conversation. I do believe there is such a thing as trying to get too much out of a story when it is no longer there – this was one such occasion.

You have read of my admiration for the manner in which Superintendent Bennett and Superintendent Fielding handled the whole outrageous incident at the Forward Command Post for the 24 hours after the shootings.

The Tasmanian community was fortunate to have such men available on that Sunday to handle the situation as it unfolded. They were also not able to say anything publicly about what they did on that day until Bryant had been through the legal system.

However, fortunately they did sit down and write about their experience for the December 1996 edition of the *Police Association News*. In the interest of fullness and perhaps give their dedication and experiences of that day a wider audience, I include their accounts in this work.

"Supt. Barry Bennett and Supt. Bob Fielding were the Forward Command for the Port Arthur massacre that took place in April this year. From their improvised

headquarters at the Taranna Wildlife Park these officers had the unenviable task of co-ordinating staff and controlling the police response to that disaster. They talk to Jenny Fleming about the difficulties associated with such a task.

"Barry Bennett – 'About lunchtime on Sunday, 28th April, 1996, I was going to a barbecue with my wife when I received a call to contact the Communications Centre as there had been a shooting. I phoned the centre and was put through to the Major Incident Room and spoke to Assistant Commissioner Prins, who said he had some information that five people had been shot at Port Arthur and could I come back in to work. I immediately drove back into Police HQ and spoke to Mr Prins, I asked who had gone to Port Arthur and he said Inspector Wild had headed in that direction. As it is in my police district (Eastern) I told him that I would be going straight away to Port Arthur to take charge of the incident down there and that he should obviously get in support to help him in the major incident room.

"'When I left, because I have an unmarked car, I borrowed a revolving flashing light from the uniform people and drove to Taranna, 10 km north of Port Arthur. On the way down Channel Six was being used for the incident and it was really overloaded with traffic coming and going. The local channel was being used for general police duties. On the way I was asking questions like 'where are the SOG?' (Special Operations Group), 'Where are the negotiators?' because they are a basic resource for the police forward commander. Everything was still very sketchy at that stage, and that was when I could get a word in on the radio; it was pretty busy.

"'I eventually got down to Taranna Devil Park where some young constables had taken over the office and started to set up the Forward Command Post with the concurrence of the owner John Hamilton, who I must say was absolutely wonderful to us throughout the whole incident. His family made coffee and sandwiches throughout the night and provided everything that he could possibly get for us at every opportunity.

"'When I arrived there was already a road block just south of the Devil Park at the Nubeena turn off. There were three telephone lines at the Devil Park, but no police radios. I parked my car as close as I could get it to a window, with the window open with a police officer sitting in my car so at least we had some radio communications. Immediately it was apparent that we were going to have problems with general communications – mobile telephones and cellular telephones did not work in the area. Our radio network was very scratchy and very poor – there was only one channel, Channel Six, so we got one constable to dial the major incident room with one of the (landline) telephones from Taranna and from that time that telephone was left off the hook and monitored so that at least we had landline contact with Hobart.

"'The police presence started to build up as we got more people in. Det. Insp. Warren arrived and I asked him to go to the incident site and take charge of the detectives *and the investigation. Inspector Freeman arrived and I tasked him with the security of the incident site. That is the historic village and where the bodies were and so forth. I was requesting more people, more general duties police, more uniform police and more detectives – so that we could start to have the place secured and could start talking to witnesses.*

"'The number of police built up over a period of time. We tried to set up as best we could the Forward Command Post in the Devil Park. We put some butcher's paper on the walls to run our logs and charts and we set up a couple of constables on running sheets and logs. We had a couple of police manning phones and even had a fax running when the BCI arrived later in the night. That is where they set up their intelligence cell.

"The Special Operations Group (SOG) arrived by helicopter and I briefed them on what I expected them to do. We had two young police officers in a ditch, Constables Allan and Whittle, directly in line with Seascape who were being fired on at that stage – they would be forced to remain there for the next eight hours.

"'There was some suggestion that there may be two suspects. It appeared at one stage that two gunmen or some people or hostages at Seascape were exchanging gunfire with the gunman as there appeared to be shots coming from two separate buildings. The secure radio net for the SOG did not work at all in the area so realistically later in the night for me to be in charge of the SOG on the ground, the only way I could communicate outside of the

open channel, obviously there were lots of things I needed to talk to them about that needed to be secured – I had to get a police officer to physically drive five kilometres with a message from me to SOG on the ground and bring whatever message they had back to me. Later in the night the SOG worked on three occasions to get closer to try and get better communications, but my biggest problem throughout that night remained communications.

"'I have been asked on several occasions how I felt about the number of dead, but quite frankly I was too busy doing things that needed to be done to stop and think about it. I only know that it seemed that every time I spoke to the media the body count went up. We had a lot to do. We had to set up the police forward command post, and get the criminal secured at Seascape and get our SOG people in there to try and find out what was going on with negotiations. Normally negotiations would be a resource for the police forward command post, but because of the telephone set up, negotiations commenced from the major incident room back in Hobart and any information I got from our negotiations was basically second and third hand.

"'Our SOG would normally monitor the negotiations for obvious reasons – to see if they could make some tactical decisions on what was going on inside the stronghold. They had no contact with the negotiators throughout the night so they were getting information through me third and fourth hand which really caused me some heartburn and slowed things down tremendously.

"*Very early on, the media started to build up in the car park. I got there about 3 pm and I think it was probably about 4 o'clock the first time I spoke to them. I took the decision to talk to the media candidly. I went outside and saw a Mercury reporter and his photographer, Robin Lane. Robin was the only one I knew and there must have been a dozen or so there at that stage. I said if you can get them together I will talk to them.*

"*They did come together and I spoke to them. I gave them the very scant information I had at that point and I told them if you play by some ground rules I will speak to you at very regular intervals and give you updates as they come to hand.*

"*Peter Hazelwood, from the Premier's Department (Office) arrived just as I finished that briefing and from that time on he was my media liaison officer and he did an excellent job. I had a very good run with the media and that is an area that sometimes causes us a lot of grief in sensitive situations.*

"*The number of police obviously built up throughout the night. We had a register running of police officers coming in and they were all coming through the police forward command post before they went in to do the various tasks they were given but there were a lot of police. The media scrum built up over the night – there were probably a dozen or so when I first spoke to them and probably the last time I spoke to them (about midnight) there were around 200. But I managed to speak to them on regular occasions.*

"'Once we got the SOG on the ground it was obvious that it was going to be a longer siege than we normally encounter. Having been the SOG commander for four years I really knew what they were going through. So I requested help from the Victorian SOG. This has never happened that I know of anywhere around Australia before. But in a very short period of time I had a reply that they were coming and prior to midnight around ten of them arrived on the ground, which was absolutely fabulous. They were sworn in as special constables.

"'Things started to quieten down somewhat after 1 am or 2 am. Contact with the offender at Seascape had ceased, because we now know that the battery on his handheld phone had gone flat. We tried to use several methods of radio broadcast to tell him to pick up the phone and to put a battery in the thing but nothing happened. Prior to that he was talking to SOG on and off up until about 9.30 pm. Right throughout my shift there were shots being fired indiscriminately at police postings. I charged the SOG with getting the two officers in the ditch out immediately they got there, but the information I got back from the SOG commander on the ground was that it was too dangerous to get them out during daylight. After dark they were extricated from the ditch and arrived back at the forward command post wet and covered in leeches. I told them to go home on several occasions, but like most officers that night, nobody seemed to want to go home. They all wanted to stay around and help. And I guess, I can relate to that because when Bob took over I *was a bit reluctant to leave myself.*

"'I don't know that there is a great deal more that I can say other than that the communications problems just added to the concerns and put pressure on everybody throughout the whole incident. It was a very difficult area for the operation because of the communications problems. What we had really was two incidents: One at Seascape with the SOG and technical people and the suspect contained and the other incident at the historic site where the original shootings took place and the security of that site. Two incidents with next to no communication between them at all.

"'I just can't speak highly enough of the people involved and the way they handled themselves. Quite frankly I have never been more proud of Tasmania Police in the 31 years I have been in the police force. Everyone worked under such trying conditions.

"'Bob arrived about 3 am and told me to go home. I sort of sat around for a while in case there were some things that I had missed in the briefing or something that he wanted to know and then he said that he had a grasp of it and he was ready to run and I drove home.

"'I couldn't go to sleep. I had a coffee and laid on the bed and watched all the news flashes on television. Afterwards when the offender was taken into custody, I then had a shower, got changed and went back to where it all started. It is my police district and I thought it the best place for me to be and there I spent the rest of the day.'

"Bob Fielding – 'Initially, I got the call at home to

go to the Operations Centre in Hobart. When I arrived I was then told to go to the Forward Command Post and take over from Supt. Bennett. I drove to Taranna and got there a little after 2 am. For a while Barry was very busy as you can imagine, he was still trying to get intelligence organised and the forward command post fine-tuned. So as is my habit in such matters I started to brief myself by walking around the forward command post looking at the status boards and talking to some of the staff. At a later time Barry had time to sit down with me very briefly and we then went into a detailed debriefing of the situation.

"At about 3.30 am I officially took over from Barry as the forward commander. As is also the practice, Barry stayed around for a little while just in case something arose that we had not covered in the briefing and by about 3.45 am I told him it was about time that he went – he was reluctant to go, naturally – and I said I didn't want to see him back before 4 in the afternoon.

"'Obviously our thoughts at that stage were that we had it contained and the main objective was to negotiate the safe release of the hostages if in fact they were still alive. That was the primary objective – to keep him contained and not to allow the situation and incident to escalate any further and to negotiate the release of the hostages. That was being frustrated to some degree because the negotiators had lost contact with him. As the manager of the incident you need to be able to talk to the hostage taker and open some form or dialogue.

Now that was not possible.

"'Prior to his portable telephone battery packing it in they were negotiating reasonably successfully with him I think. Certainly that is what the logs show. So one of the primary objectives when I took over from Barry was to continue and try to establish negotiations with him again. The property is cut off by a very large ditch or creek and the only access for any wheeled vehicle is across a small bridge that gives access to the house from the roadway.

"'The control cables for the 'echidna' which was being considered for use, stretched only 300 metres – but there was nowhere to hide an operator and then be able to safely negotiate the echidna with some equipment, either another telephone or some other form of communication, with the person in the house.

"'Those things were still being investigated right up until, I suppose daylight, and we were still trying to find a solution then. In fact some of the people responsible for that move were actually forwarded to the house endeavouring to find another means of getting some communication to him. We had difficulty as Barry has already outlined to you with having to use a police communications system which was over an open channel and the fact that we only had one channel available to us in that particular area because of its location – the actual terrain itself made communications very, very difficult.

"'We had thankfully, by the early hours of the morning, established a line between the SOG strongholding area and the police forward command post. That meant that we could talk securely with the forward elements of the SOG through their holding area back to the forward command post so there was some security in that regard with our conversations.

"'They had to move twice to try and find better communications and sustain the connection. The final holding area of the SOG was in the middle of the Arthur Highway. They were actually on the bitumen with all the gear set up because it was the best means of communications! The location prior to that was in a disused chicken shed with all the chicken manure and they all stunk of it. They were not very impressed!

"'So we were still getting those things organised when I took over the forward command post. I was very pleased with the set up, it was an ideal forward command post. It had all the things that you need: adequate parking, phones, faxes, shelter, food supplies. It would have been better if it was closer (to Seascape) but given the terrain there was nowhere else and its position was good.

"'Because it was a tourist location it had a couple of sets of toilets, male and female – at one stage we must have had a couple of hundred people at the location all using these public toilets. As you can imagine, the inevitable happened – blocked toilets. We can smile now but it was a bit of a problem at the time and we had to get them fixed.

"'Those things continued on, we continued to brief the press on a regular basis and we put together our *formulated plans for the resolution of the incident and I signed off on most of those by around 7 am.*

"At a quarter to eight the first sign of fire was seen from the house. That gave us some more difficult decisions. I had further discussions with the SOG liaison officer, the psychiatrist, Dr Ian Sale, and the head of the negotiation unit, Inspector Tom Tully. I went through with them what they thought was the situation as far as the hostages being alive was concerned. They of course did not know, unless they had actually been in the building you were never going to know. But they really thought that they were most likely deceased at that stage.

"'We didn't know where Pears was. Pears was the fellow that he (Bryant) abducted near the toll booth. We were still uncertain at that stage whether he was dead in the boot of the burnt out car, or in the house. We did not know in fact until Bryant had been arrested that Pears was in fact, in the house. No one could get close enough to the car prior to that to investigate.

"'There were also some difficulties in that Bryant had some sort of line vision device. Every time there was a slight movement in the area he was able to identify and indicate roughly the vicinity of where the SOG advancement and other people were. That was a grave concern to us. So that is why the strategy of just keeping him contained within there and doing nothing much else in the hours of darkness was maintained, because every time anyone either moved or there was any further movement of any kind he was continually firing shots.

"'The fire started and there was a lot of discussion as to what we should or should not do. In the finish I thought that I would not allow the SOG, given their likely casualty rates if they went forward, to approach the house. The house in fact burnt for three quarters of an hour. He was finally arrested at 8.30 am. He started the fire. There was a lot of things that went on at that particular time and there was some discussion about whether we would have to send somebody in because we might be letting people burn alive in there. At the end of the day I weighed it up on the basis that it was better to let that occur, than to needlessly risk another nine or ten people's lives to go in and that was what we did.

"'Certainly from his actions, Bryant wanted us to go in while the house was burning. Right up to within about ten minutes of being arrested, he was still firing shots from the house that was well ablaze and yelling out. He was trying to goad people to come in – he was yelling out things like come on, come and get me! Words to that effect.

"'He literally burnt himself out of the house. It started upstairs on the bay side. In the finish he was on fire outside the house and the SOG were finding it very difficult to see. You can imagine the amount of smoke that was around. He was in amongst the smoke; you could hear shots being fired at that stage. It was the ammunition in the house going off, there was over 2500 rounds in the house. So there were rounds being discharged from the heat of the fire as well as what he was firing.

"*He came outside and his clothes were on fire or someone came outside with their clothes on fire, they could not see because of the smoke exactly who it was. I would not allow them to go forward because I could not be certain from what they were telling me that it was Bryant.*

"*They tried talking to him but they could not make themselves heard because of the distance and the noise from the fire and the ammunition that was going off. In the finish he was visible and naked. They went forward and they arrested him using ballistic shields as protection.*

"*If you read the Australian, I was quoted as saying something at this stage and I was actually misquoted. In response to someone asking whether Bryant was armed I was supposed to have replied: 'He does have a weapon but it's no ***** use to him.' What I actually said to the SOG liaison officer was: 'Even if he is, let the bugger go for it...' bear in mind I am only getting this verbally – I can't see what is happening at Seascape. I said 'the only thing he's got is his ****mutton gun and that's not going to penetrate any ballistic shield, so go and get him!' Everyone burst out laughing. It was one of the few lighter moments of the night.'"*

As I said I think both Bennett and Fielding were deserving of more honours than they got for their work in the 24 hours after Bryant started murdering people.

Since April 28th, 1996, the media had had a fascination with Bryant. I doubt there was a week went past since his arrest that some organisation or other hasn't written to the Government asking for permission to interview him.

I know the media has a job to do, but cannot understand why they would think that a Government would deliberately give Bryant a publicity platform, which is just what he was wanting in the first place.

The only way it would ever possibly occur is if it were beneficial to the people who lost loved ones or were very nearly victims themselves, to hear from him and have him answer the question why?

From my knowledge of Government, the chances of Bryant being allowed to be interviewed by anyone in the media is none and nil and never; and that is how it should be.

However, that doesn't mean there haven't been some interesting attempts to interview him since he began his life sentence.

Just before the first anniversary, an *ABC* reporter got permission to go to Risdon to see how the authorities were looking after Bryant one year on.

I was away at the time this permission was granted, and as is nearly always the case, while the Government acted in good faith by permitting the prison staff to be interviewed, there was little good faith returned.

She was given a full tour of the prison complex, and specifically the hospital area in which Bryant was being held. But she saw really no more than any other VIP visitor to the complex would have, but somehow managed to go not only to air, but into print with an Inside Story piece she wrote (sold?) to the *Sunday Age* in March 1997, headed, "Meeting Martin".

Talk about squeezing it for every last drop. I am told that what actually happened was that she saw Bryant as he walked near her in the corridor and managed to turn that into "her disturbing encounter with Australia's worst mass murderer".

In my opinion, all she did by beating up her "meeting Martin" story was to give him more of the publicity he so desperately craves and which the State Government at the time was keen to avoid. But again, it was the case of a journalist coming into Tasmania from outside, doing a 'job' on the State and then leaving.

And in her desire to highlight the Bryant aspect of her visit to the prison, she seems to have forgotten to properly do her homework, because she called Dr Rory Jack Thompson, then known as Jack Newman, one of the State's most horrific murderers. Even first year cadet journalists are taught that if a person is found not guilty of murder on the grounds of insanity, as Thompson was, they are technically not guilty of murder, although still killers. A legal nicety, I know, but journalism/reporting is supposed to be about facts. For 18 years the local media got around the issue by calling him 'wife killer', much like another popular media phrase 'disgraced former detective' was used for Roger Rogerson.

Anyway, you could not imagine the amount of phone calls I got, most of them irate, from other media outlets when she actually had the *ABC* play a clip of her audio tape on which Bryant allegedly appeared as a preview to her *Sunday* program.

What she actually had was a few words from a fair distance away down the corridor; put them to air and allowed the suggestion of it being part of an interview with Bryant to develop, and all hell broke loose.

The truth is there was no interview with Bryant, although the *ABC* did have some tape with some fuzzy words from him on it, but it took until the program went to air that weekend for the other media to realise they had been had.

The first anniversary of the massacre duly arrived in 1997. The community was far from recovered, or fully moving on. There were even disputes amongst Port Arthur staff and survivors about having a ceremony to mark the incident at all.

In fact there was such a divide that when the Government acted to tear down the most obvious reminder of the murders, the Broad Arrow Cafe, there was outrage by the divided community. The Government thought it was acting on behalf of families of victims and survivors, but such was the divide the demolition had to be stopped and what wasn't already torn down was stabilised, cleaned up and remains on the Site to this day.

There has never been a handbook for anyone to know how to deal with an incident in which thirty-five people are killed on a worksite, but the Government genuinely thought it was acting in the best interests of those on the Peninsula. It could not be expected to know the intricacies and the internal divisions existing among survivors and Port Arthur staff at that time.

As for Bryant, while putting this work together and speaking to those who would know, I understand that he still has no remorse for what he did. He is sorry he is in jail, and he realises what he did was wrong.

But he does not regret, that for one day, he was so powerful that he could do exactly what he wanted and he did.

It was the guns that made him powerful and without them he is the childlike dolt that he was seen to be at his court appearances.

Prison life isn't all that easy for him, he has had his share of bashings from other inmates and still hasn't learnt to keep his mouth shut and not brag to others about what he did.

This also gets him into trouble. He had his lights punched out in the hospital one day by someone who everyone probably assumed was a hardened criminal. But they were wrong. The hiding was delivered by someone who had been sent to jail for not paying traffic fines. He was at the time in the prison hospital and for some reason decided that Martin deserved a biffing, and so gave him one.

The Rundle minority Government lasted for two years before it went to the elections on a platform of selling the Tasmanian Hydro-Electricity Corporation, basically privatising the entity, in an effort to pay off State debt.

The Labor party, under Jim Bacon, who campaigned against the sell-off, won office and inherited the Port Arthur issues. With the change of Government, my contract ended and I took the next six months off before accepting a media liaison role with Tasmania Police offered by now Deputy Police Commissioner, Jack Johnston.

The Commissioner of Tasmania Police, Mr Richard McCreadie, presented awards to many of those who were involved in the Port Arthur tragedy. I was awarded a certificate of commendation for my efforts with the media at the Forward Command Post at Taranna on the night of 28th April, 1996.

However, I missed the official presentation, which took place about the middle of 1996, because of a breakdown in communications which meant I wasn't told it was on, let alone that I was to be given a commendation.

It so happened that Superintendent Bob Fielding, was speaking at a SAC-PAV conference in Hobart early in 1998, and was kind enough to present it to me there, along with the brass oak leaf badge which came to symbolise Port Arthur.

Interestingly, in the two years after Port Arthur, a Sydney based Police Media Liaison officer, who I think flew into Tasmania on the Monday (29th) and never even left Hobart during the crisis, managed to get himself on the national speaking circuit. He delivered lectures and papers on 'Media Management at Port Arthur'. Let me tell you, I could have used him at Taranna on that 40 hour day. The events of that day affected a great many people, and it is a sad fact that some are never going to recover to the point they were before the murders.

Conspiracy theories about Port Arthur abound. They began soon after the shootings and for the next couple of years all manner of experts were proposing ludicrous ideas about the fact that Bryant was not the killer, or that he did not act alone.

The Age newspaper had a comprehensive news special in its 30 August, 1998, edition, and really sums up some of the 'theories', under the heading "A Conspiracy of Crackpots".

> *"Most of us think the Port Arthur massacre was the work of one crazed individual. But within the twilight zone of the lunar right, one man's madness is actually a global conspiracy.*
>
> *"In small suburban lounge rooms, great conspiracies are born. They spread in whispers, half truths, accelerating along the Internet's global highway, fuelled by a rag-tag army of far right organisations and feeding on suspicions of*

evil governments manipulating our everyday lives.

"The latest? Martin Bryant was a patsy and the Port Arthur massacre a United Nations plot, conceived decades ago to wrest guns from the populace, leaving us exposed to, well – that's where the next conspiracy comes in.

"One Nation has given credence to the Port Arthur conspiracy. The party's unsuccessful Northcote candidate supported it during his campaign. One Nation's Sale president and endorsed candidate for Gippsland, Mr Tony Peters, has called for a royal commission, claiming facts were suppressed.

"In Queensland, a new One Nation MP, Mr Jeff Knuth, used his maiden speech to dismiss Port Arthur as an 'excuse' to introduce extremist gun laws 'hatched in a faraway foreign capital'.

"Earlier this year, Mrs Pauline Hanson, interviewed in *Exposure*, a right wing magazine that has promoted the theory, said she was unsure if the massacre was part of an international plot. 'I cannot say what is true or not until I have all the information in front of me,' she said.

"Mrs Hanson has called for the legalisation of the weapon used by Bryant to kill thirty-five and wound twenty-two on 28 April, 1996. The gun lobby was outraged at finally losing the battle against tougher gun laws in the aftermath of Port Arthur.

"The speed with which new laws were outlined – within two weeks – caused groups such as the Sporting Shooters Association to allege a plot, prepared by the United Nations (it had previously debated the gun control issue). Behind the *plot lurked Japan, because in 1995, it had called for the UN to address the international proliferation of small arms.*

"Some also pointed to a 1987 statement by former New South Wales Premier, Mr Barrie Unsworth. After a spate of shootings and a frustrated attempt to introduce national laws, Mr Unsworth declared only a massacre in Tasmania would change that State's position.

"Enter Mr Joe Vialls, an Englishman who claims to be a retired oil industry 'trouble-shooter'. In his ordinary seaside home in a north Perth suburb, Mr Vialls, who claims his amateur ballistic investigation led to an inquiry into a 1984 terrorist shooting in London – began cobbling together a theory.

"Mr Vialls said the number of dead at Port Arthur sparked his suspicions. Bryant, intellectually impaired, was not capable of wreaking such havoc. A hardened professional was behind the massacre, he said.

"'His critical error lay in killing too many people too quickly while injuring far too few, thereby exposing himself for what he was: a highly trained combat shooter,' Mr Vialls said.

"'All of the hard evidence at Port Arthur bears the distinctive trademark of a planned 'psyop', an operation designed to psychologically manipulate the belief systems of a group of people.

"'Just like Lee Harvey Oswald in Dallas, Martin Bryant was a perfect patsy.' And the subsequent pulping of firearms left our nation 'terribly exposed' to anyone seeking to take our natural resources. All his conclusions

are based on 'hard science',' Mr Vialls said, although he has no scientific qualifications or ballistics training.

"According to Mr Vialls, the evidence is indisputable. There was no coronial inquiry as required by Tasmanian law, no ballistics reports were done, there was no evidence tying Bryant to the Broad Arrow Cafe, and his interrogation was doctored with only two thirds presented at trial.

"To the officer in charge of the Port Arthur taskforce, Deputy Commissioner Jack Johnston (also the man in charge of the original crime scene at Port Arthur when he was a Superintendent), the theories advanced by Mr Vialls are 'absolute rubbish'.

"In law, the Tasmanian coroner cannot hold an inquest once an offender has been charged with the murder. He may hold a hearing after a trial, but after reviewing all the Port Arthur evidence this was determined to be unnecessary.

"'Every minute' of Bryant's interrogation was presented to the trial, Mr Johnston said. Although a video camera broke down at one point, the audio tape continued uninterrupted.

"The claim that Bryant could not be tied to the Broad Arrow Cafe was nonsense, he said. A bag left by the gunman was identified by Bryant's associates and belongings inside confirmed as his. A tourist video of Bryant fleeing the cafe has also been authenticated, Mr Johnston said.

"'To suggest the gunman isn't Martin Bryant is absolutely ludicrous, given the sheer number of videos, eye witness accounts and forensic evidence,' Mr Johnston said.

"Despite the weight of evidence, Mr Vialls sent a series of articles to the right wing magazine, The Strategy. Edited

by retiree Mr Ray Platt, the paper pushes a range of political and religious theories, including that lesser races are plotting "the destruction of our gene pools and seed stocks". Published out of Mr Platt's study in the backstreets of Bendigo in 1997, The Strategy ran a story, "Was He Really A Lone Nut Assassin?" which has turned into a six part thesis.

"In the sort of coincidence that normally sets conspiratorialists abuzz, that same week Executive Intelligence Review, the magazine of American fruitcake, Lyndon LaRouch, published a radically different theory.

"Bryant was, in fact, a highly trained assassin brainwashed in the 1970's by a secret society of psychiatrists based out of the American Tavistock Institute, creating an Australian-style Manchurian Candidate.

"According to EIR, respected psychiatrist, Dr Eric Cunningham Dax was 'deployed' to Tasmania, where he briefly saw Bryant. Bryant then had secret, high level military training to enable him to carry out the massacre. The proof: 'On one of his trips to the UK he checked into a hotel in Hereford, the super sensitive home of Britain's elite Special Air Services.'

"The Motive (apparently was to) 'shell shock' and then control a population. EIR tells us Port Arthur was the latest Tavistock conspiracy following the assassinations of JFK, Martin Luther King, the Vietnam War and the Iranian hostage crisis.

"'The Tavistock-sponsored form of blind terror, of which Bryant is an example, has the great advantage to its authors that its programmed zombies almost invariably *kill themselves',* EIR *wrote.*

"This theory proved too far out for even the far right, but Mr Vialls' assertions continue to gain currency among informal extremist networks. On the internet, *The Strategy's* website is linked to the news service of Mr Scott Balson. Mr Balson runs One Nation's website and members are urged to subscribe to his Australian News of the Day. Subscribers then get free on-line access to *The Strategy.*

"Via these electronic pathways, One Nation members have received constant updates on the Port Arthur theory, which they eagerly repeat at available opportunities. One Nation director, Mr David Oldfield, told *The Age* that the party did not support the conspiracy theory, but claimed the tragedy had been cynically used by the Prime Minister to effect 'pre-planned' changes to gun laws.

"The Minister for Justice, Senator Amanda Vanstone, said One Nation's 'ramblings' made a mockery of the memories of those who died. 'I am appalled that anyone could suggest the response to the Port Arthur tragedy was anything other than a genuine response to community demand for stricter firearms controls,' Senator Vanstone said.

"Despite the continued gun lobby railing against the changes, some retain scepticism about the conspiracy. The Queensland president of the Firearms Association of Australia, gunshop owner Mr Ron Owen, describes Mr Viall's theories as 'fairyland stuff'.

"While questioning the Howard Government's motives and planning for the gun law changes, Mr Owen said the

Vialls theory did not equate with his knowledge of firearms. 'As a ballistics expert he'd make a good car washer,' Mr Owen said."

This was all happening a bit over two years since the original crime, and even today more than 20 years on, there are people out there who know Martin Bryant didn't do it.

After I started work with the Tasmania Police Service in February, 1999, I came across another of those coincidences of life.

At the start of this work I mentioned Rory Jack Thompson, and visiting him in jail.

It turns out that Richard McCreadie, the then Commissioner of Tasmania Police and my boss, was the detective who in fact questioned, and charged Rory with the murder of his wife.

On a road trip to the West Coast a few months after starting work with the police, I mentioned my 'knowledge' of Jack Newman and we had an interesting discussion about how and why I started visiting him in prison.

The Commissioner then offered some advice. Not to feel sorry for him at all, in any way, because he (Richard) knew exactly what had happened to Maureen Thompson, and that was not something for which anyone should feel sorry for Rory. What Newman did was kill his wife, cut up the body and tried to flush the pieces down the toilet.

You just never know what paths you cross in life, do you?

It was three years after the massacre in April, 1999, that Bryant's defence counsel, John Avery, revealed some of the conversations he had with Bryant in prison after taking over the case from David Gunson upon Bryant's not guilty plea at his first Court appearance.

In the *Bulletin* magazine that month he released details of a tape recording he made at the time.

"*Bryant – Will it be a long time for someone what's done...?*

Avery – You're not going to ever leave here mate, I don't think.

Bryant – Mmmmm.

Avery – You know that, don't you? I mean I would be kidding you if I said you were going to get out of here in five years or ten years or whatever. You're going to have to start putting your mind as to what you're going to do here for the rest of your life. Whether it's basket making...

Bryant – There's lots of activities here.

Avery – Or sewing up the policemen's trousers or whatever, I don't know. That's something you've got to wrestle with, right? I mean, you've got a mind. You can start thinking of what you're going to do."

And a little later: *"Avery – we are going to be frank with each other and not set any unreal expectations. I'm not going to come in here and say you are going to be out next year. You won't be home having rabbit stews with mum, I can tell you that.*

Bryant – No fear, if a person murders one person, I think they get about 21 years.

Avery – Right, well you're charged with murdering thirty-five – what's that give you ... 700 years. If we cut that in half what's that, 350. So you are not going to get out are you? You're going to have to get very friendly with these warders because they are going to retire before you are even an old man.

Bryant – at least they are being kept in a job, that's one thing.

As for remorse – this is what he told Avery; *Avery – and were you conscious of how many people you were shooting or not. Were you counting the persons?*

Bryant – no, I just looked around and thought this is the best place to sit, next to the Oriental couple, because they were all spread round that way. I thought I'd sit here and move myself round that way. It happened so quickly I just got, I just started shooting.

Avery – right.

Bryant – I shouldn't laugh.

Avery – you shouldn't what, sorry?

Bryant – I shouldn't laugh.

Avery – why do you laugh?

Bryant – otherwise you will think that I'm silly. I'm not getting anything when I laugh.

Avery – why do you laugh when you say that? Is it just a defence mechanism or is it something you feel is funny? I mean you tell me.

Bryant – I suppose I feel that it's funny, yes.

Avery – and what made you decide on this weekend, or this particular day, any significance?

Bryant – well, it was a couple of days before that I thought, 'Well, I can actually go down, kill the Martins and kill a lot of other people. I've got the guns together.' I bought

the guns, the shotgun and the AR15 and I thought I won't worry about waiting another week to get my automatic fixed up, I'll go down.
Avery – and do it.
Bryant – yeah – it was a nice day."

And so that is how Martin Bryant saw the world a few days before he was jailed forever.

I feel sorry for those custodial officers at the prison who have to look after this piece of humanity. They are largely forgotten in all of this yet have to face this person every working day of their life.

As time moved on, the Port Arthur theories, conspiratorial or otherwise, did not want to go away.

The Hobart *Mercury* reporter, Ellen Whinnett, had an extensive report in the 3 March, 2001 edition of the paper.

> *"A Port Arthur massacre survivor has publicly challenged the circumstances surround the slaying of thirty-five people.*
>
> *"Wendy Scurr, a former Port Arthur guide who survived the massacre and went on to give first aid to the injured, said she believed something was 'very badly wrong' in the official version of events surrounding the 1996 massacre.*
>
> *"The first survivor to ever expound such views publicly, Mrs Scurr, 55, of Kempton, said yesterday she was not a conspiracy theorist because 'what I know is fact'. She will make a special guest appearance later this month at a national forum organised by Australia's far right movement*

to discuss her views.

"Mrs Scurr's statements come a week after a public outcry forced One Nation leader Pauline Hanson to categorically deny Port Arthur conspiracy theories. The theories expounded by some One Nation and far right supporters and detailed in a book by West Australian man, Joe Vialls, argue gunman Martin Bryant was not responsible for the massacre.

"However, Mrs Scurr said she was not necessarily supporting those theories. 'Joe Vialls left himself open to be called a conspiracy theorist,' Mrs Scurr said.

"'What I know is fact. I don't know if Bryant did it or not, I didn't see him do it. I know I was shot at and I know certain things have happened since which are absolutely terrifying.'

"Mrs Scurr said she believed something was 'very badly wrong' with the official version of events. 'The 90-second theory they put out in court is wrong,' she said.

"'For Bryant to kill thirty-two people with twenty-nine bullets in 90 seconds, that's impossible, it's crap. I was there and it took four or five minutes. I don't hold one view or another on Martin Bryant, but if it was done in 90 seconds, that wasn't Martin Bryant, that was a sharp shooter'.

"Mrs Scurr said she did not advocate calls for a royal commission, but believed a coronial inquiry should be held. 'We know where, we know how, but we don't know why,' she said."

Wendy went on later that month to speak at the Inverell Forum in NSW, an event organised by a group of Australia's far-right organisations. She was speaking alongside Victorian man Andrew Mcgregor on the topic: "Port Arthur, Deceit and Terrorism".

Twelve years after Port Arthur, Bryant's lawyer, John Avery was back in the news, but for all the wrong reasons.

The Mercury newspaper, 08 September, 2008, had this story:

"Avery talks of Martin Bryant hangover", and they weren't subtle.

"Crooked lawyer, John Avery felt his life changed after acting for Port Arthur gunman Martin Bryant, a court has heard.

"The Supreme Court in Hobart heard today there was intense media pressure on Avery during the three month period he acted for the multiple murderer.

"'He found the pressures of the media on him was enormous,' said Avery's lawyer David Gunson SC. (Yes, Hobart is a very small place. Mr Gunson was the original Counsel for Bryant.)

"Avery has described his life after the case as akin to an AFL footballer going back to playing for a country team. Avery has pleaded guilty to 130 counts of stealing and dishonesty between December, 2001, and March, 2006, while a director at the Moonah law practice, Avery Partners.

"The 60 year old stole more than $500,000 from clients and his law firm partners. Mr Gunson confirmed that 'Avery's compulsion to acquire art had overtaken his sense of judgement. His desire to obtain cutting edge art became an acquisitive zeal,' he said.

> "'Mr Avery accepts that he lived beyond his means'. But he said 'Avery had never deliberately sought to hurt any of his clients. He held a naive belief that he was not ripping off his clients' he said.
>
> "'He acknowledges that he took more than his fair share. He said Avery was unable to pinpoint a reason or time when things went out of control.
>
> "'Mr Avery's appearance here represents what can only be described as an extraordinary fall from grace,' he said."

Two weeks later Avery was sentenced to 4 ½ years jail with a non parole period of two years and three months. This sentence was successfully appealed and the *Mercury* newspaper reported his resentencing on 1 May, 2009. Again they were not subtle.

> "Thieving lawyer John Avery will be locked up for longer after an appeal against the length of his sentence was upheld today.
>
> "Last September Avery was sentenced by Chief Justice Ewan Crawford to 4 ½ years in jail with a non parole period of two years and three months after pleading guilty to 130 counts of stealing and misappropriation. The former Moonah based lawyer stole more than $500,000 from clients and his former practice over more than five years to pay for his lavish lifestyle and love of art, until he was busted by an employee in 2006.
>
> "This morning the Court of Criminal Appeal increased Avery's sentence to six years, with a non parole period of four years.

"The Director of Public Prosecutions, Tim Ellis, told the court Avery had been almost truculent over the issue of repaying his victims and had made no proposal for reimbursement at the time of his sentencing."

The next year Avery voluntarily petitioned to become bankrupt owing more than $1.3 million. I don't know if Avery and Bryant have actually crossed paths in Risdon Prison.

I have been a shooter all my life. Growing up in the bush of far western New South Wales, as kids you are taught how to safely use firearms. We learnt they were tools on the farm, not toys, and they were never considered so.

During the Federal Government firearms buyback after the Port Arthur murders, I lost all my guns. A .30 calibre M1 semi-automatic carbine, built in the General Motors Factory in America during 1942, an Erma .22 calibre semi automatic and a Mossberg pump action shotgun.

The anti-gun lobby would have me and fellow gun owners portrayed as 'killers in waiting' because I owned those particular firearms. To this day I resent the inference and I know hundreds of thousands of law abiding firearm owners feel the same way.

While I understand why the Government banned certain firearms because I saw firsthand what happened at Port Arthur, the anti-gun lobby insists on besmirching anyone who owns a firearm. They no doubt will continue their campaign until there are no firearms owned by the general public. Make no mistake that is their ultimate aim.

Sadly, and it is a truism, Government's can legislate for the lunatic, and on this day in April, 1996, that was what the country was dealing with.

The general public in Australia will never again have access to the now banned automatic and semi automatic long arms. The challenge for legal firearm owners into the future is to ensure that the laws as they currently exist (2017) are not unfairly tightened even further.

I think that at this time, the balance is right. We are not America and should not be compared to what happens there because of their laws.

In the last 20 years I have heard all the dozens of conspiracy theories. I believe them to be rubbish and don't deserve a response. The person who killed the thirty-five people at Port Arthur is behind bars, he acted alone, and will only come out of Risdon Prison in a coffin.

And it might interest readers to see how I was caught up in these conspiracy theories. You have just read in the previous pages how I thought I was involved in the Port Arthur massacre and its aftermath.

Please now read what was published on one of many internet websites by people who obviously knew more about what I was doing than I did.

"This is Peter Hazelwood the Media Officer to the then Premier Ray Groom in 1996 at the time of Port Arthur. (I was actually the Head of the Government Media Office under Premier Groom who was the Premier immediately before Tony Rundle.)

"He attended at the police forward command post at Taranna when the Seascape siege was running. Hazelwood

was also reportedly the Media Liaison Officer at the Hilton Hotel Bombing (in Sydney) back in 1978 which was later found by a Royal Commission to have been orchestrated by persons connected with ASIO. He just happened to be the duty media officer that day.

"Peter, a shadowy figure during and after Port Arthur, is believed to be an intelligence officer for a federal government agency. This site believes this man can shed a lot of light on what happened at Port Arthur that day (but noting this site does not believe he was the instigator of it).

"Following the massacre Peter hung around survivors of the Broad Arrow Cafe shooting advising them what to do and what not to do – picking up information. He reportedly tried to vet what those people should say in response to media questions and advised them to say nothing of what they knew claiming it would interfere with Martin Bryant's trial (which never occurred). Strange behaviour for the Premier's media officer. All of this was to try and keep a tight lid on the facts of what went on that day so it would not derail their agenda. His associate, Geoff Easton, believed to be another intelligence agency officer, was the Tasmanian Police Media Officer at the time, and this (web) site believes he too could shed even more light on the massacre.

"The 1978 Sydney Hilton Hotel bombing, for those who are not aware of its details, involved a bomb being planted in a garbage bin outside the Sydney Hilton resulting in several people being killed. Following the media frenzy the incident was used to justify more powers for ASIO and other Canberra based organisations, which this site *believes were used in setting up the Port Arthur massacre and were also behind the other high profile gun massacres in Australia in recent years – Hoddle and Queen Street in 1987 (Melbourne) and Strathfield in Sydney in 1991 and the attempted massacre at the Melbourne abortion clinic.*

"Like Port Arthur the authorities blamed a third party – the Ananda Marga Sect for the Hilton bombing. Like the ASIO powers following the Hilton bombing, Port Arthur similarly resulted in more power for those in law enforcement. Those in law enforcement in Tasmania and Canberra were the same people who investigated this incident and have covered up what when on – a state of affairs akin to placing an arsonist in charge of the fire department.

"A summary of the Hilton incident and those behind it was contained at the following web address, and you will see the similarities. (I haven't included the address in the interest of the reader's sanity.)

"The above picture of Hazelwood was taken by a Broad Arrow Cafe survivor following suspicions about his activities. Hazelwood nearly always appeared in dark clothes and wearing face concealing sunglasses. (I should say here that this picture is how "Hazelwood" looked when he attended the emotional private memorial service for Port Arthur victims on the historic site on the Friday after the shootings in 1996, because that's when it was taken.)

"If these men were in fact intelligence officers for Federal agencies what were they doing masquerading as media officers at the time of the Port Arthur massacre? The answer needs no explanation."

And so there it is, I am now a federal agent, or at least in the eyes of these clowns who no doubt eat conspiracy theories for breakfast.

Almost every year since 1996 there has been a service to mark the shootings at Port Arthur. Some have been organised by the Government or the Historic Site, some have been simply organised by survivors and families.

Each year the wounds seem to be re-opened and the healing process delayed yet again for those most affected. And every year since 1996, (until I left Tasmania in 2005) I have gone back to the site for the memorial service, but without really understanding why I was doing so.

I now realise it was to show support for John and Sue Burgess who lost their teenage daughter Nicole on that day of madness.

Although I never knew Nicole, or John or Sue before April, 1996, (I first met them five days after the shootings at the Memorial service at the Historic Site) I feel a great affinity for them.

I also feel a great indebtedness to them for graciously agreeing to let me dedicate this personal observation of Port Arthur and the events of 1996 and the following years to their daughter.

Sadly, John died 29 May, 2014, aged 65. He is buried at St. Alban's cemetery, Koonya, next to Nicole.

Four years after the massacre in the year 2000, it was finally decided what form the official memorial on the site would take. It was hoped that this would see an end to much of the division that has existed in the local community since April, 1996.

The memorial garden is a lasting tribute to those who died, and about a thousand people attended the ceremony in April,

2000, to officially dedicate it.

The shell of the Broad Arrow Cafe remains as a constant reminder to those who know what happened on 28 April, 1996. Although for a long time, feelings on the Peninsula were such that visitors were discouraged from asking Port Arthur staff about that day.

However, there is now an official brochure of information which is made readily available to those who ask about the day. Somehow, I feel more is needed.

It is now more than 21 years since that dreadful day. Australians are not generally morbid, but I believe there is a genuine interest by visitors to the Historic Site in knowing what happened that afternoon.

After all this was an Australian tragedy. I personally saw and felt the national outpouring of goodwill that flowed to Tasmania in the wake of the shootings and think the memory of the thirty-five who died demands ongoing recognition and honouring of their lives and indeed death.

ABOUT THE AUTHOR

Peter Hazelwood started a journalism cadetship with radio station 2GB in Sydney in 1969. Over the next nearly twenty years he worked variously in the newsrooms of 2UW, 2SM, 2WL, 2CH and again at 2GB, before moving to Tasmania in 1988.

For the next 18 years he worked as a Government press secretary, as political editor for the Advocate newspaper for three years, ran a Government media office, served as press secretary to a Premier and was media advisor to the Police Commissioner and Tasmania Police.

Returning to Sydney in 2005, he worked in short term Government Departmental contract positions before being appointed senior advisor to the Shooters Party members of the New South Wales Parliament where he worked for nearly ten years.

His motivation for writing this account was the fact that no similar work has been produced in which the author was so closely involved with the incident for so long. He felt there was a need, even 20 years on, to have the details within this work placed on the public record.

He currently lives in Brisbane with his wife, Kristen.

www.ingramcontent.com/pod-product-compliance
Lightning Source LLC
Chambersburg PA
CBHW071903290426

44110CB00013B/1261